Zion and Bryce Canyon

Trivia

Don Lago

RIVERBEND
PUBLISHING

FOR DAVID AND GERRY,
WITH THANKS FOR YOUR
GREAT COMPANY ON OUR
GRAND CANYON-ZION
BRYCE CANYON
ADVENTURE)
APRIL, 2016

ACKNOWLEDGMENTS

My deepest thanks go to Marker Marshall for her faith in me and this project, and for her knowledgeable company on Zion and Bryce Canyon trails. Thanks to Janet Spencer for shepherding this book; to Wayne Ranney for his geological depths; and to Warren Ueckert for his decades of Zion experience. Jan Stock and Ron Terry improved this book with their experience and suggestions. Both parks have excellent ranger staffs who contributed their knowledge. At Zion: Caitland Ceci, Amy Gaiennie, Adrienne Fitzgerald, Barbara Graves, Robin Hampton, Ron Kay, Sarah Stio, Leslie Courtright, Holly Baker, Robert Eves, Mike Large, Letitia Lussier, and Rosalie Ellsworth. At Bryce Canyon: Kevin Doxstater, Kevin Poe, Cheryl Evans, and Gary Battel. Greer Chesher quote from *Zion Canyon: A Storied Land,* © 2007 Greer K. Chesher, reprinted by permission of the University of Arizona Press.

Zion and Bryce Canyon Trivia
© 2011 Riverbend Publishing; text © 2011 Don Lago
Published by Riverbend Publishing, Helena, Montana
ISBN 13: 978-1-60639-036-8
Printed in the United States of America.

1 2 3 4 5 6 7 8 9 SB 15 14 13 12 11

Cover design by Ron Trout
Text design by Barbara Fifer

Riverbend Publishing
P.O. Box 5833
Helena, MT 59604
1-866-787-2363
www.riverbendpublishing.com

CONTENTS

INTRODUCTION: TWO CHAPTERS OF THE SAME STORY

It makes a lot of sense to combine Zion and Bryce Canyon in the same book.

For starters, Zion National Park and Bryce Canyon National Park are neighbors, and most visitors tour both parks.

More importantly, Zion and Bryce Canyon have a great deal in common. They are part of a larger story. They are both on the Colorado Plateau. They are both part of the Grand Staircase. They were both formed by the same geological forces. Their wildlife and plant life have much in common.

Of course, Zion and Bryce Canyon do have differences. Zion has the tallest sandstone cliffs in the world. Bryce Canyon has the best hoodoos in the world. By comparing Zion and Bryce Canyon and seeing why their geology turned out differently, you can understand both of them better. Their differences are variations of one story, the story of the Colorado Plateau. Most of the famous national parks of the Southwest—including the Grand Canyon—are part of the Colorado Plateau, and your experience of all of these national parks will be richer if you can see "the big picture."

Zion and Bryce Canyon also share a great deal of human history, including their Native American cultures, their Euro-American explorers, and their Mormon pioneers. Zion and Bryce Canyon inspired the same artists. The same architect designed the lodges at both parks.

Combining two national parks into one book does require a word of explanation about how the material is organized. The material is organized by theme, such as geology, history, or adventures. Chapters begin with Zion material, and conclude with Bryce Canyon material, although many entries mention both parks. However, the chapter on astronomy is mostly about Bryce Canyon. The chapter on culture is organized into subjects such as movies, architecture, and art, with the Zion and Bryce Canyon material combined under each subject.

GEOGRAPHY
THE MOST BEAUTIFUL LANDSCAPES ON EARTH

Q. Zion and Bryce Canyon are two chapters of the Colorado Plateau story. What is the Colorado Plateau?

A. Geographers divide the United States into 25 "geographic provinces" that have distinct landscapes. Other well-known geographic provinces include the Rocky Mountains, the Great Plains, and the Basin and Range. The Colorado Plateau includes 130,000 square miles (336,700 sq km) in the Four Corners states—Utah, Arizona, New Mexico, and Colorado. The Colorado Plateau was named for the Colorado River, which is its main landscape feature.

Q. The Colorado Plateau contains some of the most famous and beautiful landscapes on Earth. Many of these landscapes are preserved as national parks. How many national parks are there on the Colorado Plateau?
1) Five   2) Seven   3) Nine

A. 3) Nine: Zion, Bryce Canyon, Grand Canyon, Arches, Canyonlands, Capitol Reef, Black Canyon of the Gunnison, Petrified Forest, and Mesa Verde. There are also many national monuments, including Cedar Breaks, Canyon de Chelly, and Natural Bridges. The Colorado Plateau makes up only 3 percent of the area of the United States, but it holds 15 percent of America's national parks. The Colorado Plateau has more national parks than the states of California and Alaska, each of which has eight (more than any other state).

Q. Why does the Colorado Plateau have so many amazing landscapes?

A. Its rocks! You don't need to know anything about geology to enjoy the beauty of the Colorado Plateau, but the rocks are trying to tell you some amazing stories. The Colorado Plateau consists of a three mile (4.8 km) deep layercake of rocks, mostly sandstone and limestone. These rocks record nearly two billion years of time—nearly half the age of Earth. Nowhere else on Earth is the geological record so well preserved. You can't see this entire three miles of rock in any one place, since it is spread out, tilted, and chopped up. When you stand on the rim  of Bryce Canyon, you are standing on the top of this layercake. When you look into the bottom of the Grand Canyon, you are seeing the bottom portion. When you stand in Zion Canyon, you are seeing the middle.

Q. Most of the national parks of the Colorado Plateau share the same theme. Elsewhere, other national parks have other themes. Great Smoky Mountains and Grand Teton national parks are all about mountains. Sequoia and Redwood national parks are about trees. Other parks are about caves, volcanoes, deserts, or archaeology. What is the theme of the national parks of the Colorado Plateau?

A) Erosion
B) Earthquakes
C) Sandstone

A. 1) Erosion. It has carved deep canyons like Zion Canyon and the Grand Canyon, and carved exotic rock formations like the hoodoos of Bryce Canyon, the arches of Arches National Park, and the natural bridges of Natural Bridges National Monument. At every park and monument, the erosion has turned out differently.

National parks make up three percent
of the area of the United States.

Q. Why does the Colorado Plateau have so much erosion?

A. It starts with sedimentary rocks like sandstone and limestone, which erode into dramatic shapes and colors. These rocks were created in or near ancient seas. Much later, these rock layers were lifted out of the seas to become land. The Colorado Plateau was lifted especially high. At Bryce Canyon, you are more than 8,000 feet (2,438 m) above sea level, and even on the floor of Zion Canyon, you are more than 4,000 feet (1,219 m) above sea level. The land has to have a high elevation before it can have deep canyons carved into it. You also need a "knife" to carve those canyons, and the Colorado River is a powerful knife. The tributaries of the Colorado River have to drop a long way to meet the river, and this steep drop gives them a lot of carving power. One of those tributaries is the Virgin River, which carved Zion Canyon.

Colorado Plateau outlined

Zion and Bryce Canyon are located on the western edge of the Colorado Plateau, which is its highest edge. The Colorado Plateau consists of many smaller plateaus, and the western edge is called the "high plateaus of Utah." Zion is part of the Markagunt Plateau, and Bryce Canyon is part of the Paunsaugunt Plateau (both these words are Paiute words).

Q. True or false: While Zion's Kolob Canyons are on the Colorado Plateau, the Kolob Canyons Visitor Center, which is only a few miles away from Kolob Canyons, is not on the Colorado Plateau.

A. True. When you drive from the Kolob Canyons Visitor Center and up the steep road to the Kolob Canyons, you are climbing onto the very edge of the Colorado Plateau. The Kolob Canyons were created by creeks that drop steeply off the edge of the Colorado Plateau. Zion Canyon is about twenty miles (32 km) inside the Colorado Plateau, but it too was carved by water that is dropping over the edge of the plateau. Similarly, when you drive from

285 million people visit America's national parks every year—
16 times the total that attends NFL football games.

Cedar Breaks to Cedar City on Highway 14, you are dropping off the edge of the Colorado Plateau.

Q. Zion and Bryce Canyon are part of "the Grand Staircase." What is this?

A. On the western side of the Colorado Plateau, the layers of rock form a series of tall cliffs and long slopes. In the 1870s, explorers John Wesley Powell and Clarence Dutton began referring to these cliffs and slopes as a "great stairway." Originally, this term referred only to the cliffs above the rim of the Grand Canyon and north of it, mostly in Utah. But over time, geologists began using the term "Grand Staircase" to include the rock layers inside the Grand Canyon. The term "Grand Staircase" is still used in both ways, which could be a bit confusing.

Top of the Grand Staircase, Bryce Canyon, looking north from Rainbow Point.

The cliffs of the stairway are named for their colors. In ascending order, the cliffs above the Grand Canyon are the Chocolate Cliffs, the Vermillion Cliffs, the White Cliffs, the Gray Cliffs, and the Pink Cliffs. The Pink Cliffs are what you are standing on at Bryce Canyon. The White Cliffs are the layers that surround you in Zion Canyon. When you stand at Bryce Canyon's Rainbow and Yovimpa points and look south, you can perceive this series of cliffs dropping away from you. When you are descending Highway 89A from the North Rim of the Grand Canyon toward Zion or Bryce Canyon, you will get some stunning views looking up the Grand Staircase to your north.

Q. The heart of Zion National Park is Zion Canyon, the deep sandstone gorge that includes the Virgin River, Angels Landing, the Riverside Walk, and Zion Lodge. How long is Zion Canyon?

A. Nearly nine miles (14 km). Zion Canyon is measured from the mouth of the Narrows to the park boundary near the Visitor Center. Beyond that, the cliffs open wide. More than two-thirds

---

Many national parks have grown over decades. Zion is twice its original size, and Bryce Canyon is three times its original size.

of that nine miles is covered by the Zion Canyon Scenic Drive. In length and depth, Zion Canyon is similar to Yosemite Valley, but it is narrower, and while Yosemite is made of granite, Zion Canyon is made of sandstone.

Nothing can exceed the wondrous beauty of Zion Valley... in its proportions it is about equal to Yosemite, but in the nobility and beauty of the sculptures there is no comparison.
—Clarence Dutton, 1882

Q. How deep is Zion Canyon?
A. This is a bit tricky to answer, since it depends on where you are measuring from. The bottom isn't hard to find: the Visitor Center is at 3,923 feet (1,196 m), and by the end of the Zion Canyon Scenic Drive, you've climbed several hundred feet.

It's the top of Zion Canyon that has more variation. The tallest point along the canyon is West Temple, which is 7,810 feet (2,380 m) high, or 3,887 feet (1,184 m) higher than the Visitor Center. The Great White Throne, at 6,744 feet (2,055 m), is 1,066 feet (325 m) lower than West Temple. Angels Landing, at 5,990 feet (1,825 m), is another 754 feet (230 m) lower; it's about 1,900 feet (519 m) higher than Zion Lodge. The rim of the canyon has lots of peaks, slopes, and dips. If you average all those together, it's fair to say that Zion Canyon is 2,000–2,500 feet (609-762 m) deep.

Q. For comparison, let's define Zion Canyon as 2,500 feet (762 m) deep. If you took Lake Superior, the deepest of the Great Lakes, and placed it inside Zion Canyon, would it reach the rim?
A. No. Lake Superior is 1,330 feet (405 m) deep, so you would need nearly two Lake Superiors to reach the top of Zion Canyon. The deepest lake in the United States is Crater Lake at 1,932 feet (589 m), still shallower than Zion Canyon.

Q. If Niagara Falls was falling into Zion Canyon, how many times farther would it need to fall to reach the bottom of Zion Canyon?
1) Three times   2) Seven times   3) Fourteen times
A. 3) Nearly 14 times farther. Niagara Falls is 182 feet (55 m) tall. Zion Canyon has many waterfalls taller than that, although most of Zion's waterfalls flow only after storms or during spring snowmelt.

A majority of visitors at Zion and Bryce Canyon are first-time visitors.

Q. The Great Pyramid of Giza was the tallest of the seven wonders of the ancient world. How many pyramids could you stack up inside Zion Canyon?

1) Two
2) Five
3) Ten
A. 2) Over five. The Great Pyramid of Giza is 481 feet (146 m) high.

Q. If you placed America's tallest building, Chicago's Willis Tower (formerly the Sears Tower), into Zion Canyon, would it reach the rim?
A. No, the people on the top floor of the Willis Tower would still be looking up at the people on top of Angels Landing. The Willis tower is "only" 1,451 feet (442 m) tall.

Q. If you stacked the Washington Monument, Seattle's Space Needle, and the St. Louis Gateway Arch on top of one another, would they reach the top of Zion Canyon?
A. No. The Washington Monument is 555 feet (169 m) tall, Seattle's Space Needle is 605 feet (184 m) tall, and the St. Louis Gateway Arch is 630 feet (192 m) tall. Together they would add up to 1,790 feet (604 m), still well short of the rim of Zion Canyon.

Q. The highest elevation in Florida is 345 feet (105 m). How many Floridas could you stack up like pancakes inside Zion Canyon?
1) Three
2) Seven
3) Fifteen
A. 2) Over seven.

Q. How narrow is the Zion Narrows?
1) 100 feet (30 m) wide and 500 feet (152 m) deep
2) 50 feet (15 m) wide and 750 feet (228 m) deep
3) 16 feet (5 m) wide and 1,000 feet (304 m) deep
A. 3) At one point, it is 16 feet (5 m) wide and 1,000 feet (304 m) deep.

---

*Highway 9, from La Verkin to Zion, zigzags just to avoid
the lone grave of a pioneer.*

Q. How large is Zion National Park?
A. 148,753 acres, or 232 square miles (601 sq km). Of 58 national parks, Zion ranks 36th in size. Of course, you can't measure scenic beauty by mileage.

Q. What are the highest and lowest points in Zion National Park?
A. The highest point is Horse Ranch Mountain, at 8,726 feet (2,660 m). The lowest is Coal Pits Wash at 3,666 feet (1,117 m). This makes a difference of over 5,000 feet (1,524 m). When you drive from the south entrance (Springdale) to the east entrance (Checkerboard Mesa), you are gaining about 2,000 feet (609 m). These differences in elevation create lots of different habitats for plants and wildlife.

Q. What's the hottest temperature ever recorded at Zion National Park?
1) 105 F (40.5 C)
2) 110 F (43 C)
3) 115 F (46 C)
A. 3) 115 F (46 C), in July, 2002. That's close to the hottest temperature ever recorded in the state of Utah: 117 F (47.2). That's hotter than the highest temperature ever recorded in Florida: 109 F (42.7 C). The hottest month at Zion is July, with a normal daily high of 100 F (37.8 C). The normal daily low for July is 68 F (20 C). In August the normal daily high is 97 F (36 C), and in June it's 93 F (33.8 C). In all, Zion has 109 days per year with highs above 90 F (32.2 C).

Q. What's the coldest temperature ever recorded at Zion National Park?
1) 6 F (-14.4 C)
2) 2 F (-16.6 C)
3) -15 (-26.1 C)
A. 3) -15 F (-26.1 C), in January, 1937. The coldest month at Zion is January, but the normal daily high is still 52 F (11.1 C), the low 29 F (-1.6 C). Zion has 74 days per year when the temperature drops below 32 F (0 C).

Q. What are the wettest and driest months at Zion National Park?
A. Winter months get the most precipitation, much of it in

The red pavement on Zion Canyon roads is made from volcanic cinders, meant to blend in with the red cliffs.

the form of snow. March is the wettest month, with 1.7 inches (4.3 cm) of precipitation. January and February have 1.6 inches (4 cm). August also gets 1.6 inches (4 cm), during the summer thunderstorm season. In all, Zion gets 14.4 inches (36.6 cm) of precipitation per year. This is 2 inches (5 cm) less than Salt Lake City, but 6 inches (15.2 cm) more than Phoenix, Arizona. Zion gets less than one-third the precipitation of New York City.

Zion's all-time record for one year was 25.9 inches (65.7 cm), in 1978; and its all-time low for one year was 3.2 inches (8.1 cm), in 1956.

The driest month is usually June, with 0.6 inches (1.5 cm). One definition of a desert is any place that loses more moisture through evaporation than it gains from rain and snow. At Zion, evaporation outdoes precipitation by about four to one.

Q. When Zion first became a national monument in 1909, it was called Mukuntuweap (moo-koon-too-weap) National Monument. Where did this name come from?
A. According to explorer John Wesley Powell, this was the Southern Paiute name for Zion, meaning "straight canyon." Stephen Mather, the first director of the National Park Service, felt that "Mukuntuweap" was an awkward name, so in 1918 he was happy to change it to "Zion," the name local settlers had used for decades

Q. Who first named it "Zion"?
A. A pioneer named Isaac Behunin, who was a member of the Church of Jesus Christ of Latter-Day Saints, commonly called the Mormons.

The word "Zion" started out as the name of one of the hills on which Jerusalem was built. Over time, this name came to represent Israel as a whole, then the idea of a place of sanctuary or a promised land. The Mormons had been driven out of the American Midwest by religious persecution, and they saw all of Utah as their place of sanctuary, their Zion. To Isaac Behunin, the walls of Zion Canyon were more than just a safe fortress: "A man can worship god among these great cathedrals as well as in any man-made church."

The name "Utah" came from a Native American tribe, the Utes.

Q. Who named the rock formations in Zion Canyon?

A. Many of the most prominent features were named in 1916 by Frederick Vining Fisher, a Methodist minister who lived in northern Utah. Fisher was accompanied by two local youths. They

named the Three Patriarchs, the Great White Throne, the Organ, and Angels Landing—"only an angel could land on it." The Great White Throne already had a name: "El Gobernador," or "the Governor," named for a governor of Utah, but Fisher felt that Zion's grandeur called for more inspiring names. For him, the Great White Throne was the throne of God: "I have looked for this mountain all my life but never expected to find it in this world."

Angels Landing

Fisher was continuing a long tradition of seeing religious grandeur in western landscapes. Geologist Clarence Dutton had filled the Grand Canyon with the names of temples from many religions.

As European immigrants settled the vast American continent, they needed many thousands of names for new towns and for the landscape. Sometimes settlers adopted Native American names, such as "Massachusetts." Before the American Revolution, settlers honored European places and royalty, such as "New York" and "Virginia." As the new American nation acquired its own history, Americans named places for presidents, war heroes, and explorers. Quite often, places got named for the first person to settle there. This was the case with Bryce Canyon, named for the pioneers Ebenezer and Mary Bryce, who lived there only five years before moving to Arizona. In contrast with Native Americans, who had ancient connections with the land and meaningful names for it, Americans often filled the land with names that had only fleeting, superficial connections with it. But with Zion Canyon, Americans were inspired to come up with names with a greater meaning. The place names in Zion National Park come from many sources. Some are Native American names, such as Mt. Kinesava and the Temple of Sinawava, named for Paiute gods. Many names invoke religious grandeur, including

Garfield County, which includes Bryce Canyon, is so rural it doesn't have any traffic lights.

Cathedral Mountain. Some names honor pioneers, such as Behunin Canyon. Many names are descriptive of the landscape, such as Checkerboard Mesa, Emerald Pools, and Echo Canyon. Some names reflect flora and fauna, such as Cougar Mountain and Grapevine Wash. And it seems that Zion has a lot to hide: there's Hidden Canyon, Hidden Arch, Hidden Gardens, Mystery Canyon, Mystery Falls, and the Mountain of Mystery.

Q. How did the "Altar of Sacrifice" get its name?
1) The red mineral streaks on it look like blood.
2) It is shaped like an altar in a church.
3) It was going to be sacrificed for a sandstone quarry, but the National Park Service altered those plans.
A. 1) Its red streaks looked like blood.

From left: Zion's West Temple, The Sundial, and the Altar of Sacrifice.

Q. "The Sundial" is the name of one of the peaks of the Towers of the Virgin. How did it get its name?
1) It has a sharp spire, like a sundial.
2) The residents of the town of Grafton set their clocks by when the first morning sunlight hit it.
3) It holds big mineral stains that look like numbers.
A. 2) The residents of Grafton set their clocks by it.

Zion's "The Watchman" was named because it guards the entrance to Zion Canyon.

Q. How did Refrigerator Canyon (on the Angels Landing Trail) get its name?
1) One winter, pioneers found a dead bear frozen there.
2) Hikers to Angels Landing often "get cold feet."
3) Its narrow depths get almost no sunlight, leaving it cool even in summer.
A. 3) Its narrow depths stay cool even in summer.

Q. The South Campground is north of the Watchman Campground, so why is it called the South Campground?
A. The South Campground was named in relation to Zion's original campground, which was located north of it, in the Grotto.

Q. The national forests around Zion and Bryce Canyon are called the "Dixie National Forest," and many other things in southern Utah are named "Dixie." Why is this?
A. In pioneer days, Mormon leaders set up cotton-growing colonies in southern Utah, with settlers from the southern U.S., since they knew the most about growing cotton.

Q. The river that runs through Zion Canyon is the Virgin River. How did the river get this name?
A. Native Americans called this river "Pa'rus," which means a rushing, turbulent stream. When the Spanish explorers Dominguez and Escalante encountered the Virgin River in 1776, they called it the Sulphur River for nearby hot sulphur springs. In the 1820s American fur trapper Jedediah Smith called it the Adams River after President John Quincy Adams. One theory holds that the name "Virgin" came from one of Smith's men, Thomas Virgin. Another theory holds that Spanish traders named it for the Virgin Mary.

At least we can say where the river itself begins. It comes from a spring near Navajo Lake (near Cedar Breaks National Monument). Actually there are two branches of the Virgin River, and they meet just downstream from Zion National Park. In all, the Virgin River is about 160 miles (257 km) long, and it empties into the Colorado River—now Lake Mead.

Q. Most of the waterfalls in Zion Canyon flow only in the springtime, when snow is melting, or they flow briefly after

---

Zion's Deertrap Mountain was named for how Paiute hunters herded deer into a trap in the landscape.

a summer rainstorm. One exception is the waterfall at the Emerald Pools, which stops only in a bad drought year. One time the waterfall at the Temple of Sinawava suddenly went from flowing with clear water to flowing black. Why was this?
A. A forest fire on the plateau above had created lots of ashes, which got into the stream and colored it black.

Q. What was the first nation to establish a national park?
1) The United States   2) Switzerland   3) Sweden
A. 1) The United States. Yellowstone became the world's first national park in 1872. National parks are "America's best idea," and a very democratic idea: that natural wonders belong to everyone, not just the rich and powerful. America's national parks have inspired dozens of nations to create their own national parks.

Q. How many people visit Zion National Park every year?
1) 1.6 million   2)   2 million   3) 2.6 million
A. 3) 2.6 million, or more. This ranks Zion in the top ten national parks. About 25 percent of Zion visitors are from outside the United States, at least in summer; the top five countries of origin are France, Germany, England, the Netherlands, and Italy.

Of American states, California provides about 25 percent of Zion visitors, with Utah second. Only 10 percent of Zion visitors visit the Kolob Canyons section of the park. Bryce Canyon National Park gets over 1.5 million visitors per year; park rangers estimate that Bryce Canyon is the #1 national park in the percentage of its visitors that are from outside the United States—about 50 percent.

Q. The Wilderness Act of 1964 provided that areas be set aside as nature made them, as habitats for wildlife, not for human use, not even for roads. In 2009 a portion of Zion National Park was designated as wilderness. What percent?
1) 16 percent   2) 32 percent   3) 84 percent
A. 3) 84 percent.

It would take more than a lifetime to really know Zion; but in a week you might really know yourself. And that's even better.
—Freeman Tilden

Zion's Temple of Sinawava was named for the same Paiute god who turned the Legend People into Bryce Canyon's hoodoos.

Are you a "looking up," or a "looking down" person?

The national parks of the Southwest offer two kinds of experience. At some parks you are standing on the rim of a canyon and looking down into it. At other parks you are standing at the bottom of a canyon and looking up at cliffs. Bryce Canyon is a "looking down" experience, as is the Grand Canyon. Zion is a "looking up" experience, as is Yosemite. Many people discover that they prefer one experience over the other.

Looking down on a canyon is mostly a visual experience, offering sweeping vistas and large patterns. Looking up can be a more emotional experience, offering a deeper sense of personal immersion. Famous landscape artists have had their preferences.

Georgia O'Keefe was a "looking up" artist, seeking an intimate experience with the land, focusing on flowers or bones in the foreground and leaving the cliffs in the background. Though Georgia O'Keefe lived for decades within 300 miles (482 km) of the "looking down" Grand Canyon, she never painted it. Maynard Dixon painted Zion many times, but painted the Grand Canyon only once. By contrast, Gunnar Widforss spent his life painting the Grand Canyon. The book *A Century of Sanctuary: The Art of Zion National Park* includes over 100 paintings of Zion, and almost all of them are "looking up" from the canyon floor. One of the few exceptions is a Widforss painting that looks down from the rim. For him, this was how canyons are supposed to look.

Q. True or false: Bryce Canyon isn't really a canyon.
A. True. As geologists define canyons, a canyon is carved by a river.

Bryce Canyon is actually the edge of a plateau, which has eroded through

Zion's "Three Patriarchs" are three peaks named for biblical figures Abraham, Isaac, and Jacob.

weathering. Geologists define Bryce Canyon as an "amphitheater." More accurately, it's a long series of amphitheaters. Canyons have two rims, but Bryce Canyon has no opposite rim. It might have been better to call it "Bryce Breaks," like Cedar Breaks. "Break" is an old word for a plateau edge that has "broken" into a badlands landscape. Still, from the edge of Bryce Canyon you are looking down 1,000 feet (304 m) or more, deeper than many canyons. Zion, of course, is very much a canyon, but it isn't called "Zion Canyon National Park," simply "Zion National Park."

Q. Bryce Canyon is famous for its "hoodoos," its colorful and weirdly shaped rock spires. Where did the word "hoodoo" come from?
1) From the word "voodoo."
2) It is an acronym for the geological term "Horizontally Order-Optimized Dendritically Oddified Objects."
3) Bryce Canyon's hoodoos are the favorite nesting place for the western midnight owl, whose eerie call is "hoooo-doooo."
A. 1) It comes from the East African word "voodoo," which came to America with slaves and became the name for a Caribbean form of magic. Bryce Canyon's hoodoos seemed magical.

Q. Bryce Canyon's most famous hoodoo is called Thor's Hammer. What was it named for?
1) Explorer Thor Heyerdahl, whose hammer saved his raft *Kon-Tiki* from sinking
2) The Norse god of lightning and thunder
3) Thor Gagarin, a gold medalist in the Olympic hammer throw
A. 2) The Norse god of lightning and thunder, Thor. Thor made lightning and thunder by striking his mighty hammer. The day Thursday was named for Thor. Thor is an appropriate name for Bryce Canyon, since Bryce Canyon gets lots of lightning. Other hoodoos are named for the architecture they resemble, such as "the Cathedral" and "Tower Bridge," and some are whimsical, such as "the hat shop."

Kolob Canyons was designated a national monument in 1937, and added to Zion National Park in 1956.

In Southern Paiute legend, the hoodoos of Bryce Canyon were once the Legend People, who looked like people but who were really many kinds of animals and birds. The Legend People were selfish and greedy, stealing food from others. Even coyote, the trickster god, grew tired of their greed, and as punishment he turned them into stone. At the moment this happened, some of the Legend People were standing, some were sitting, and some had red paint on their faces, and that's the way they remain today. At night, you may be able to hear their moans and sobs at being imprisoned in stone.

Bryce Canyon's hoodoos are a feast for the imagination. You can see all sorts of shapes in them: people, animals, or famous architecture. Some people see Elmer Fudd chasing Bugs Bunny, or Marge Simpson watching a TV. The hoodoos are like a Rorschach test, inkblots onto which people project their own thoughts. For much of the 1800s it was popular for poets to compare nature with fantasy objects like giant's castles or fairy gardens. When geologist Clarence Dutton saw Bryce Canyon in the 1870s, he saw "the work of giant hands, a race of genie once rearing temples of rock." This tradition lives on in the hoodoo section called Fairyland. When Bryce Canyon National Monument was dedicated in 1923, the ceremonies played up the fairy theme, with children dressed as fairies. The Union Pacific Railroad promoted Bryce Canyon as "fairy cities in painted stone."

Yet among poets and nature writers, this type of symbolism went out of style long ago. As nature writer Edward Abbey put it: "I see more poetry in a chunk of quartzite than in a make-believe wood nymph...than in whole empires of obsolete mythology." While it is fun to see all sorts of shapes in the hoodoos, the rocks have their own story to tell, a geological story full of deep time and amazing events.

12 percent of summer visitors to Zion make voluntary donations to the park.

Q. Bryce Canyon lies on the boundary between two major watersheds. Rain that falls onto the hoodoos flows to the east, into the drainage system of the Colorado River, which includes 244,000 square miles (631,957 sq km) and empties into the Gulf of California. What happens to rain that falls onto the parking lots just west of the hoodoos?
1) It flows into the Pacific Ocean.
2) It flows into the Great Basin.
3) It flows into the Mississippi River.
A. 2) It flows into the Great Basin. The Great Basin is a large area of the American West where rivers find no outlet to the sea. Instead, rivers empty into lakes, and water evaporates. The best-known of these lakes is the Great Salt Lake. The Great Basin includes half of Utah and most of Nevada. One of the dividing lines between the drainages of the Colorado River and the Great Basin is the rim of Bryce Canyon. As you walk from the parking lots at Sunset or Sunrise points to the rim, you are walking slightly uphill. This little slope is all it takes to send water flowing away from the rim and to the west, where it joins the Great Basin.

Q. Many photographers consider Bryce Canyon to be the most photogenic of any national park. Bryce Canyon's red and pink rocks glow with brilliant colors and subtle reflections and shadows. Most photographers will tell you that Bryce Canyon is at its best at one time of day. Which time?
1) Sunrise   2) Midday   3) Sunset
A. 1) Sunrise. At both sunrise and sunset, sunlight has to travel through more atmosphere than at midday, and this brings out the redder part of the light spectrum. When you mix red light with Bryce Canyon's red rocks, it makes the red colors especially rich. Since Bryce Canyon's hoodoos face east, the direction of sunrise, the light penetrates the hoodoos more at sunrise than at sunset. The point of a Bryce Canyon sunrise isn't to look at the sun itself, but to watch the play of light and color on the rocks.

Q. The most popular Bryce Canyon overlooks are Sunset Point, visited by 83 percent of park visitors, and Sunrise Point, visited by 76 percent of visitors. Did Sunrise Point and Sunset Point get their names because they are the best places to see sunrise and sunset?

Both Zion and Bryce Canyon national parks award about 10,000 Junior Ranger badges every year.

A. Not really. They were named at a time when almost all visitors to Bryce Canyon arrived by tour bus and stayed at Bryce Canyon Lodge and had to walk to the rim. It would have been a long walk to Bryce Point, the overlook that to-day's rangers usually recommend for the best sunrises. From Bryce Point you get a wider view of the hoodoos. Also, from Sunrise or Sunset points, you and your camera are looking into the glare of the rising sun.

From Sunrise Point

Q. How large is Bryce Canyon National Park?
A. 35,835 acres, or 56 square miles (145 sq km). Bryce Canyon National Park is 18 miles (29 km) long, but it's skinny, only five miles (8 km) wide at its widest point.

Q. What is Bryce Canyon's elevation?
A. At the Visitor Center, you are at 7,894 feet (2,406 m). This is nearly 4,000 feet (1,219 m) higher than the Visitor Center at Zion National Park. At Bryce Point you are at 8,331 feet (2,539 m). At Rainbow Point, the highest point in the park, you are at 9,115 feet (2,778 m). The lowest point in Bryce Canyon National Park is 6,620 feet (2,017 m). As a general rule, with every 1,000 feet (304 m) in elevation that you gain, you lose about 4 degrees in temperature, so Bryce Canyon is usually about 20 F (11 C) cooler than Zion Canyon.

Q. True or false: In its entire history, Bryce Canyon National Park has never recorded a temperature of 100 F (37.8 C).
A. True. The hottest temperature ever recorded at Bryce Canyon was 97 F (36.1 C), which is 18 F cooler than Zion's record high of 115 F (46.1 C). In the months of December, January, and February, Bryce Canyon's highs have never hit 70 F (21.1 C.)

Q. In an average year at Bryce Canyon, how many days does the temperature rise above 90 F (32.2 C)?
1) 5   2) 52   3) 102

An early proposed name for Bryce Canyon was
"Temple of the Gods National Monument."

A. 1) Only five! By contrast, Zion has 109 days per year when the high is above 90 F (32.2 C).

Q. What was the lowest temperature ever recorded at Bryce Canyon?
1) -10 F (-23.3 C)   2) -20 F (-28.9 C)   3) -30 F (-34.3 C)
A. 3) -30 F (-34.3 C). This is 15 F colder than Zion's all-time low of -15 F (-26.1 C). In July Bryce Canyon's record low is 25 F (-3.8 C), and in August it is 17 F (-8.3 C).

Q. In an average year at Bryce Canyon, how many days of the year is the low temperature below 32 F (0 C)?
1) 126   2) 176   3) 236
A. 3) 236. By contrast, Zion has an average of only 74 days a year below 32 F (0 C). As we'll see in the geology chapter, Bryce Canyon's freezing weather plays an important role in the creation of its hoodoos.

Q. In an average year, which park gets more precipitation, Zion or Bryce Canyon?
A. Bryce Canyon gets 16.3 inches (41 cm) of precipitation, and Zion gets 14.4 inches (36 cm). Much of Bryce Canyon's precipitation comes in the form of snow. Bryce Canyon has received traces of snow even in July and August, and in both February and March it has received 75 inches (190 cm) of snow, or over 6 feet. Bryce Canyon averages 54 thunderstorms per year, while Zion averages 46. Bryce Canyon's higher elevation produces its higher precipitation.

Q. From Bryce Canyon overlooks, most of the land you are seeing belongs to one national monument. Which one?
1) Cedar Breaks   2) Grand Staircase-Escalante   3) Pipe Spring
A. 2) Grand Staircase-Escalante National Monument, which stretches about 60 miles (96 m) to Lake Powell (Glen Canyon

*Ebenezer and Mary Bryce's cabin is now on display
in the town of Tropic.*

National Recreation Area). Grand Staircase-Escalante, with 1.9 million acres (768,905 hc), is the largest national monument in the United States outside of Alaska. Its rocks hold one of the best fossil records in the world, especially of dinosaurs.

Q. The book stores in the park visitor centers are run by the Zion Natural History Association and the Bryce Canyon Natural History Association. What are these?

A. Most national parks have a "cooperating association" that is responsible for selling educational materials to the public. This idea started in Yosemite in 1923. The National Park Service (NPS) was a new agency with a small budget and lots of needs, but it was prohibited from raising money directly from the public. Lovers of Yosemite got together to raise money to help the NPS build a museum. By the year 2000 the nation had 65 cooperating associations, which raised $112 million annually, donated $26 million directly to the NPS, and used millions more for their own educational programs and publications.

The Zion Natural History Association, founded in 1931, was one of the first cooperating associations. It donates over half a million dollars to Zion National Park every year; in 1984 it donated the new visitor center at Kolob Canyons. The Bryce Canyon Natural History Association was founded in 1961 and has helped Bryce Canyon National Park remodel its visitor center and fund the Junior Ranger program. Both associations operate field institutes that offer classes led by experts.

A spring near Zion Lodge was long called "Menu Falls" because its photo appeared on the lodge's menu.

GEOLOGY
THE BEAUTY SECRETS OF ROCKS

Geology can be a bit abstract and confusing, so let's start by hearing the wonder of geology expressed by an ordinary cowboy. Well, maybe he's not the most ordinary cowboy. In the movie *Electric Horseman*, Robert Redford plays a cowboy who steals a champion horse from a Las Vegas casino, where the horse is being drugged to make it perform on stage. Redford takes the horse back to the wild, where he feels it belongs. In fact, Redford takes the horse to just outside Zion National Park. Redford explains why he is amazed by Zion: "This whole land was under water millions of years ago. If you go slow, take your time and you look real close, you can find skeletons of these *weird*-looking fish...long, long gone. And all these mountains, and everything, everything you can see, everything was under an ocean." That's the fun of geology: if you look real close, the rocks will tell you some amazing stories. You don't need to understand geology to enjoy the beauty of Zion and Bryce Canyon, but behind that beauty, there are the secrets of why Zion Canyon has the world's tallest sandstone cliffs, and why Bryce Canyon has the world's best hoodoos.

Q. Robert Redford's character wasn't entirely correct about one thing. While most of the rock layers of the Colorado Plateau were deposited under the ocean or at shallow bays or swampy shores near oceans, the rock layers of Zion Canyon and Bryce Canyon are both exceptions. Where were these rocks deposited?
1) In a desert   2) In a lake   3) Zion Canyon's rocks were deposited in a desert, and Bryce Canyon's in a lake.
A. 3) Zion Canyon's Navajo Sandstone was deposited in a desert, and Bryce Canyon's rocks were deposited in a lake. Both types of rocks are sedimentary rocks, which are made up of tiny sediments like sand (which becomes sandstone), mud and silt (which becomes shale), or biological material (which becomes limestone). The special conditions in which the rocks of Zion and Bryce Canyon were created has a great deal to do with why Zion's cliffs and Bryce Canyon's hoodoos turned out so special.

Q. The tall red cliffs of Zion Canyon and of the Kolob Canyons are one thick layer of sandstone called Navajo Sandstone. It is as thick as 2,200 feet (670 m), which is about twice as thick as the thickest rock layer in the Grand Canyon. Sandstone is made out of sand. The sand in the Navajo Sandstone was once part of the sand dunes of a huge desert called the Navajo Desert, about 190 million years ago. How do we know this sand was part of desert sand dunes?

A. You can see it! The cliffs are full of lines, little sloping and crisscrossing lines, called "crossbedding." These are the outlines of ancient sand dunes. When wind is piling up sand grains into dunes, it forms slopes and curves. When the sand turns into sandstone, these shapes are "frozen" into stone. The dunes you see in Zion's cliffs have the same outlines as the dunes you'd see in a desert today. The Navajo Desert had massive sand dunes, as tall as 150 feet (46 m), like today's Sahara Desert. When you look at Zion's cliffs, you can tell which way the wind was blowing 190 million years ago.

---

*Zion and Bryce Canyon don't contain precious metals
like gold or silver.*

We worked our way up through time. Each step consumed a thousand years...In Zion Canyon you are engulfed in time. Time below you, time above you, time laid down beside you in miniscule grains of sand...
—Lyman Hafen, *Mukuntuweap: Landscape and Story in Zion Canyon*

Q. How big was the Navajo Desert?
A. Big! It's the largest desert preserved in the geological record anywhere on Earth. It was at least 150,000 square miles (388,500 sq km), covering most of the Colorado Plateau and spreading into California, Wyoming, and southern Arizona. Zion National Park includes the deepest, central part of the Navajo Desert.

Q. Where did all the sand of the Navajo Desert come from?
A. It was coming out of rivers draining from the Appalachian Mountains, which were much larger than today. An era of severe drought encouraged the formation of a large desert.

Q. The Navajo Sandstone forms unusually tall and smooth cliffs. Why is this?
A. The Navajo Sandstone is a uniform rock, made of the same stuff from top to bottom, and this means it erodes at a uniform pace. If the Virgin River had been hitting a series of harder and weaker rocks as it cut Zion Canyon, it would have cut into the softer rocks faster and deeper, and left Zion Canyon as a series of slopes and cliffs. Also, the Navajo Sandstone is a strong rock that can support the weight of 2,200 feet (670 m) of cliffs.

Q. The Navajo Sandstone's cliffs are white on top, and red below. Why are there different colors?
A. The red color results from iron oxide. The tops of the cliffs don't have much iron. Geologists are still debating why. One theory is that the top layer never had much iron to begin with. Another theory is that the top once had iron, but the iron got washed away by rain seeping into the rocks or by natural gases escaping upward.

When traveling to southern Utah for the first time, it is fair to ask if the redrocks were cut, would they bleed.
—Terry Tempest Williams

The word "plateau" comes from the French word for tray, implying a flat top.

Q. Like today's deserts, the Navajo Desert had oases: pockets of water, plants, and animals. In an oasis with a lake, lots of plants and shells and bones piled up in the lake, and one day these sediments turned into limestone, a little lens of limestone surrounded by huge amounts of sandstone. On the Canyon Overlook Trail, you walk through such a lens of limestone. These ancient oases are the only place in the Navajo Sandstone where you are likely to find something. What?
1) Fossilized coconuts
2) Dinosaur footprints
3) Springs

A. 2) Dinosaur footprints. About 160 sites with dinosaur footprints have been identified in Zion National Park. You could call Zion "Jurassic National Park," for the Navajo Sandstone formed in the Jurassic Age. But you aren't likely to find dinosaur footprints in the sandstone itself, because sand doesn't preserve footprints the way mud does. Other rock layers in Zion National Park include lots of fossils, fossil footprints, and petrified wood—some of this petrified wood was washed there from 200 miles (322 km) away.

Grallator dinosaur (related to modern storks and herons) and its footprint.

Q. Eventually, the sand dunes of the Navajo Desert turned into sandstone. True or false: Sand or other sediments are turned into stone when so much weight piles up, it pressures and heats the sediments into stone.

A. False. The sediments are "glued" together by minerals seeping through them. Eventually, the Navajo Desert was covered by the ocean, and water from it seeped into the sand and bonded it together.

Q. Did the Navajo Sandstone get its name because Navajos once lived at Zion?

A. No. Geological layers are named for the location where geologists first identified them. Many of the rock layers of the Colorado Plateau

For the last five million years, the Colorado Plateau rose at a rate of 730 feet (222 m) per million years.

were first identified on Navajo lands in northeast Arizona. The layer below the Navajo Sandstone is the Kayenta Formation, named for a Navajo town near Monument Valley. Below the Kayenta formation is the Chinle Formation, named for a town at Canyon de Chelly. But the layer just above the Navajo Sandstone is called "the Temple Cap Formation," and it was identified in Zion Canyon, and got its name because it caps Zion's temples. (Note: To geologists, a "formation" is a layer of one type of rock, while the popular term "rock formation" means rocks eroded into interesting shapes.)

Q. After the Colorado Plateau was lifted high above sea level, its rocks began to erode. What was the agent of erosion at Zion and Bryce Canyon?
1) Water   2) Wind   3) Glaciers
A. 1) Water. While Zion is often compared with Yosemite, which was carved by glaciers, there weren't any glaciers at Zion. Water's erosive power can be violent, as when the Virgin River floods; or very quiet, as when water seeps into Bryce Canyon's rocks and freezes and cracks the rocks apart.

Q. How old is Zion Canyon?
1) 100,000 years   2) two million years   3) 50 million years

A. 2) About two million years old. Geologists estimate that the Virgin River has been cutting the canyon at a rate of 1.3 feet (0.4 m) per thousand years, or over 1,000 feet (304 m) in one million years. This means that one million years ago, Zion Canyon was only half as deep as it is today. The Narrows was not yet there, although there could have been another set of Narrows farther downstream from where they are today. Over time, erosion has been cutting farther and farther back into the Markagunt Plateau. Millions of years ago, there could have been a Narrows where the town of Springdale is today. The

Sedimentary rocks make up 5 percent of Earth's crust, but 75 percent of rocks exposed on Earth's surface.

Virgin River isn't finished cutting into the Markagunt Plateau; the river could cut Zion Canyon another 1,000 feet (304 m) deep.

Q. But how could a little river like the Virgin River cut such a deep canyon? If the Virgin River was back east, it might be called a creek.
A. The Virgin River gets its erosive power from its gradient. Falling water has a lot of energy. The Virgin River is a very steep river. In 160 miles (257 km) it falls more than 7,500 feet (2,286 m). It falls 48 feet per mile. Within Zion Canyon, it falls 76 feet per mile. This is more than ten times steeper than the drop of the Colorado River within the Grand Canyon. This is 120 times steeper than the drop of the Mississippi River.

Q. Another factor that gives the Virgin River its cutting power is its sediment, its sand and silt, which acts like liquid sandpaper against the rocks. The Virgin River is a very dirty river. It carries about one million tons of sediment per year. The mighty "Big Muddy" Mississippi River carries 245 million tons of sediment per year, so the tiny Virgin River is carrying 0.4 percent of that. To visualize one million tons of sediment, let's picture it in terms of African elephants, which weigh about seven tons. How many elephants worth of weight is the Virgin River carrying every year?
1) 12,379 elephants 2) 86,494 elephants 3) 142,857 elephants
A. 3) 142,857 elephants per year. This works out to 391 elephants per day, 16 elephants per hour, and one elephant every 3.7 minutes. If you measured this in terms of blue whales, the largest mammal on Earth, the Virgin River is carrying about one blue whale every hour. And that's just the weight of the dirt in the water, not the weight of the water itself.

Q. The Virgin River gains even more erosive power when it floods. Let's imagine a flood in which the river's volume goes up ten times. When the volume goes up ten times, how much more sediment does the river carry?

Rivers carry only one-millionth of Earth's water.

1) 10 times more   2) 300 times more   3) 2,000 times more
A. 3) 2,000 times more. The river's higher speed gives it a lot more energy to lift and carry sediments and to erode rocks. The Virgin River does most of its canyon carving during floods. In an average year, 15 days of floods may do as much carving as the other 350 days combined.

Q. Zion Canyon is a lot wider than today's Virgin River. True or false: the Virgin River was once as wide as the canyon.
A. False. The Virgin River you see today is probably about the same size it was a million years ago. The Virgin River has cut only the depth of the canyon. The width of the canyon was cut by rain and streams and waterfalls pouring over the cliffs, and by landslides. As erosional debris falls into the canyon, the river carries it away like a conveyor belt. Yet the Virgin River has been cutting downward faster than the sides of the canyon are eroding. All the side streams that empty into Zion Canyon are trying to cut to the level of the Virgin River, but they can't keep pace with the river's cutting, so Zion Canyon is full of drainages that "hang" far above the canyon floor, drainages that turn into tall waterfalls.

Q. You can't miss seeing the evidence of how Zion Canyon's cliffs are eroding. As you start up the Scenic Drive into Zion Canyon, you'll see steep, rough slopes to your left, across the river. These slopes are part of a massive landslide that happened about 7,000 years ago; it's called the Sentinel slide because this rock debris broke off of the rock tower called the Sentinel. When the Sentinel slide happened, it left a 600 foot (182 m) deep rock pile blocking the river. Behind this dam, river waters rose into a lake many miles long. This lake lasted perhaps 4,000 years. Sediments in the Virgin River began piling up in the lake. The flat bottom of today's Zion Canyon was the bottom of this lake. If you drilled down below Zion Lodge, how deep would these lake sediments go?
1) 25 feet (7 m)   2) 100 feet (30 m   3) 300 feet (91 m)
A. 3) Beneath Zion Lodge, there's 300 feet (91 m) of lake sediments. The lake's surface was 50 feet (15 m) above Zion Lodge. Eventually, the dam broke, the lake drained, and the river reestablished its course.

Zion's Pine Creek Bridge, at the bottom of the switchbacks on the Zion-Mt. Carmel Highway, contains many colors of sandstone, representing all the rock layers in the park.

Q. One night in April 1995, after a wet winter that saturated the debris of the Sentinel slide, there was another landslide there, bringing down 110,000 cubic feet of debris. This debris dammed the river and forced the river to cut into the highway. How much of the highway was wiped out?

Sentinel slide site

1) 100 feet (30 m)
2) 250 feet (76 m)
3) 600 feet (183 m)

A. 3) 600 feet (183 m). About 430 people were trapped at Zion Lodge for 22 hours. Out of fear that the dam would break and cause a big flood, the campgrounds downstream were evacuated. The road was rebuilt, but only three years later the Virgin River flooded and destroyed this section of road again.

Erosion at Zion never stops. Sometimes, it gets personal. In 1880 the arch of Red Arch Mountain, above the Grotto, was created when huge slabs of rock fell onto the farm of the Gifford family below. Luckily, the family was away at church. In 1947 a boulder weighing 880 tons crushed a parked truck. In 1975 a flash flood swept a car 150 feet (46 m) down a gully, twisting the car into a wreck, but the occupants survived. In 1994 a man was walking on the Emerald Pools Trail when he photographed a rockslide happening just above Zion Lodge. In 2005 a 700-ton boulder slid onto the Zion-Mt. Carmel Highway. In 2001 a 250-ton boulder rolled onto a house in Rockville, smashing most of the house; the owner was asleep in the part of the house that wasn't smashed. In 1992 a magnitude 5.8 earthquake sent a 3,600-foot (1,100 m) wide landslide onto several houses in Springdale and blocked the highway into the park—but no one was killed. Zion once had a rock formation called "the Sphinx," but its nose fell off and it no longer looks like a sphinx.

Regardless of how constant these canyon walls appeared on this day in this decade in this century, I was actually walking through a work in progress. There was a time in ages past when the canyon

At the end of the last Ice Age, with all the melting snow, the Virgin River was larger, for a while.

did not exist, and as long as the rain falls and the wind blows and time passes, it will continue to change. The minuscule window of our lives on earth affords us only a few precious glimpses of the brush strokes that change the picture—a rock slide here, a flash flood there...we can only count ourselves blessed to be surrounded by all the beauty that process offers.

—Lyman Hafen, *Mukuntuweap: Landscape and Story in Zion Canyon*

Q. For many visitors, the most magical places at Zion are its "hanging gardens," where water seeps out of the cliffs and creates lush gardens full of columbines and maidenhair ferns. Where is all this water coming from?

A. It is flowing through the rocks. Navajo Sandstone is a very porous rock. In between all its tiny sand grains, there's quite a bit of empty space. Rocks vary in how porous they are; granite may have only one percent empty space, while sandstone can have up to 30 percent. All this space allows water to percolate down through rocks. As you look up at the cliffs of Zion Canyon, you can see trees growing out of bare rock; the trees are tapping into the water inside the cliffs. But when water reaches the bottom of the Navajo Sandstone, it hits the Kayenta Formation, which is much less porous, so the water can't continue downward, and it flows sideways and  comes out the cliffs as springs. The Kayenta Formation makes up the slopes beneath Zion Canyon's tall cliffs. When you are walking up the Riverside Walk, you are right at the boundary between the Navajo Sandstone and the Kayenta Formation, which is why the trail has many hanging gardens.

Q. How long has the spring water of hanging gardens been underground?
1) Two years   2) 100 years   3) 1,200 years
A. 3) Hydrologists have tested the water coming out of Weeping

---

The words "erode" and "rodent" have the same Latin root: "rod," to gnaw.

Rock and found it has been underground for 1,200 years. At a nearby spring, the water has been underground for 4,000 years. When a rock layer is so porous that it can hold a lot of water for a long time, it is called an "aquifer," and the emerging water is called "fossil water." Zion National Park has several water stations where you can fill your water bottles with spring water that fell as rain when the Mayans were building pyramids and the Vikings were roaming the seas.

Q. Some people fall in love with the Emerald Pools before they see them—just because of the name. Emeralds are a green gem. Emeralds were mined by ancient Egyptians and worn by European royalty. The Wizard of Oz lived in the Emerald City. True or false: the Emerald Pools got their name because of tiny emeralds embedded in the rocks.
A. False. They were named for their green color, which is caused by algae in the water. But this color has faded due to all the foot traffic there.

Q. The cliffs of Zion Canyon are full of streaks and patches of many colors. What makes these?
A. The most widespread color is a black called "desert varnish." The desert wind is full of clay and brushes it onto cliffs, and then bacteria metabolize the clay into manganese, which is black. The varying darkness of desert varnish can tell you how long rocks have been exposed to air; when a cliff caves off, the newly-exposed patch is much lighter than the rock around it. Native Americans created petroglyphs by scratching off the desert varnish. If you see a narrow black streak beneath trees, it's tannic acid from the trees. Waterfalls leave streaks of red iron and purple manganese. Springs have white streaks where evaporation leaves minerals and salt. Green, orange, and yellow splotches on rocks are lichen. Black splotches may be moss, which turns green when rain comes.

Q. Do Zion and Bryce Canyon have earthquakes or volcanoes?
A. The Colorado Plateau is an unusually strong and stable part of Earth's crust, so it doesn't have many earthquakes. But as the plateau was uplifted, it did break into many faults, especially along its edges. These faults allowed lava to reach the surface.

Bryce Canyon is a "badlands" landscape, like Badlands, Theodore Roosevelt, and Petrified Forest national parks, and Cedar Breaks National Monument.

As you drive on Interstate 15 just west of the Kolob Canyons, or on Highway 9 a few miles west of Springdale, you can see large lava flows. There are six lava flows within Zion National Park; the most recent was 100,000 years ago, and the oldest was 1.4 million years ago. The uplift of the Colorado Plateau created billions of cracks, or "joints," in its rocks, and these cracks have made it easier for water to start erosion. In earthquakes, Bryce Canyon's hoodoos make good seismographs, since it doesn't take much shaking to break some apart.

Q. True or false: Zion's Kolob Arch is the largest natural stone arch in the world.
A. False. For years there was a friendly debate between Zion National Park and Arches

National Park over which park has the world's largest arch. Because arches have irregular shapes, it's not clear where you should take their measurements. The latest measurement places Zion's Kolob Arch at 287 feet (87 m) across. Considering that Arches National Park has 2,000 arches, and that its Entrada Sandstone is perfect for forming arches, it's amazing that Zion can compete at all.

Q. The cliffs at Bryce Canyon are full of bands of different colors. What are these?
A. These are the colors of different types of rocks. The rocks of Bryce Canyon were deposited in a large lake, which covered much of Utah about 50 million years ago. Over millions of years, about 1,000 feet (304 m) of sediments piled up in this lake. The types of these sediments changed from time to time. It might be sand, or mud, or gravel, or silt, or clay, or algae, or mollusk shells. Sometimes these different sediments mixed together, so one layer was a mixture of sand and mud, while another layer was a mixture of sand and lime. The primary rock type at Bryce Canyon is limestone. Different

---

Bryce Canyon's gullies are ten times steeper than the Virgin River in Zion Canyon.

limestone layers got mixed with different minerals, giving the rocks different colors. Manganese gives rocks their blue and purple colors, and iron oxide gives rocks their red, yellow, orange, and brown colors. The more pure the limestone is, the more white it is. The 1,000-foot (304 m) layer of rocks formed in this lake is called the Claron Formation. It contains fossils of freshwater snails and clams.

Q. Bryce Canyon's different layers of rocks are the secret of why the rocks formed hoodoos. What's the secret?

A. The different types of rocks erode in different ways. Some rocks are harder, and some are softer. The harder rocks erode more slowly than the softer rocks. If a harder layer sits atop a softer layer, then the lower rock will erode faster than the rock above it. This leaves a larger rock sitting atop a smaller column of rock. These larger, harder rocks then act like umbrellas to protect the softer rock columns from rain and further erosion. When there's a

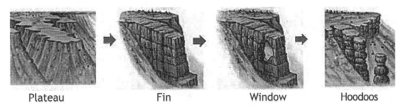

| Plateau | Fin | Window | Hoodoos |

whole layer cake of harder and softer rocks, it forms pillars with a series of fat sections and skinny sections. Eventually, pillars become too skinny to support the weight above, and they collapse.

Q. Bryce Canyon's weather played a large role in creating the hoodoos. Why was this?
1) There's lots of rain.   2) There's lots of wind.
3) There's lots of freezing and thawing.

A. 3) Freezing and thawing. Bryce Canyon has over 200 days per year when the temperature rises above freezing during the day and drops below freezing at night. In the daytime water seeps into cracks in rocks, and when the water freezes at night it expands by about 10 percent in volume and exerts a lot of pressure on the rocks, helping to crack rocks apart. Bryce Canyon's 200 days of freezing and thawing is an unusually large number, and is due to its 8,000-foot (2,438 m) elevation.

Unlike Zion, Bryce Canyon has few springs; a major exception is the Mossy Cave.

Q. To the east of Bryce Canyon lies the Table Cliffs Plateau, which at 10,000 feet (3,048 m) is the highest plateau in North America. The Table Cliffs Plateau and the Paunsaugunt Plateau, which includes Bryce Canyon, were once connected, but faulting has raised the Table Cliffs Plateau 2,000 feet (609 m) higher than the Paunsaugunt Plateau. Both plateaus are made of the same rocks, but the Table Cliffs Plateau has far fewer hoodoos than Bryce Canyon. Why is this?

A. Because the Table Cliffs Plateau is 2,000 feet (609 m) higher than Bryce Canyon, it stays a lot colder and has far fewer freeze-thaw cycles.

Q. Why are there long rows of hoodoos, with narrow canyons (like Wall Street) between them?

A. The Paunsaugunt Plateau was full of cracks, or joints. Rain-

water flowed into these joints and widened them into gullies, then gulches, then canyons. Where two canyons run side-by-side, it leaves a long, narrow fin of rock between them. These fins erode into hoodoos, and sometimes rows of windows.

Wall Street, Bryce Canyon National Park

Q. For many years, the glossy brochure handed to visitors at Bryce Canyon included a photo of a hoodoo at Rainbow Point called "the Poodle." But finally this photo was removed. Why?

1) Poodle lovers complained it was insulting to poodles.

2) The poodle had eroded so badly, it no longer looked like a poodle.

3) In accordance with its wilderness values, the National Park Service renamed the hoodoo "the Coyote."

A. 2) It no longer looked like a poodle. Erosion at Bryce Canyon never stops.

Although scientific concepts explain how hoodoos grow and colors form, nothing can quite explain the effect these geologic ele-

---

Bryce Canyon's Fairyland section is younger and less eroded than the Bryce Amphitheater.

ments have on the human mind...why a pyre of luminous rocks flickering red, orange, yellow, and white with the force of a wildfire can inspire us to dream. Only our hearts can tell us that.
—Greer Chesher

Q. Because Bryce Canyon's rocks are softer than Zion's rocks, erosion is happening faster at Bryce Canyon. How much faster?
1) Twice as fast   2) Five times as fast   3) Forty times as fast
A. 3) Bryce Canyon's cliffs are retreating at a rate of 1 to 4 feet (0.3 to 1.2 m) per century, which is from 10 to 40 times faster than the Virgin River is deepening Zion Canyon. Bryce Canyon's rate of erosion is noticeable in a human lifetime. In 2009 the sidewalks between Sunrise and Sunset points were relocated farther back from the rim, since the rim had eroded too close to the old sidewalks. But Bryce Canyon Lodge is far enough from the rim that it should be safe for 10,000 years. In another three million years, the entire Paunsaugunt Plateau will erode away.

Q. What's the most valuable tool geologists use to measure the rate of retreat of Bryce Canyon's cliffs?
1) Surveyors' instruments   2) Trees
3) NASA's Batscope satellite. "Batscope" is short for "Bryce Area Transition Spectrographic Collimator of Periodic Erosion."
A. 2) Trees. As the rim erodes, trees that had sprouted right on the rim get left hanging in the air, their roots now grasping soil a foot or more away. A good example of this is the limber pine in front of Sunrise Point. Tree-ring dating can reveal what year a tree sprouted, and this shows how far the rim has retreated since then.

Q. All the dirt that erodes from Bryce Canyon flows into the Paria River, whose headwaters are right below Bryce Canyon. The Paria River flows into the Colorado River at Lees Ferry, which is the beginning of the Grand Canyon. The Paria River carries one of the highest concentrations of sediment of any river in the world. What percent of the Paria's volume consists of sediment?
1) 10 percent   2) 25 percent   3) 50 percent
A. 3) About 50 percent. The Paria River delivers five times more sediment into the Colorado River than all the other tributaries inside the Grand Canyon combined. When you look into the Grand

The Paria River, which begins at the foot of Bryce Canyon, carved a famous set of slot canyons far downstream.

Canyon and see the muddy Colorado River below, you are seeing the remains of Bryce Canyon hoodoos!

Q. Bryce Canyon's Natural Bridge is 125 feet (38 m) tall. True or false: the Natural Bridge isn't really a natural bridge.

A. True. To geologists, a natural bridge is formed by a stream running beneath it. Bryce Canyon's Natural Bridge is really an arch. Arches are formed as cliffs decay and pieces fall off. Zion too has an arch that was mistakenly called a natural bridge; this was the origin of the name "Bridge Mountain."

The state fossil of Utah is a dinosaur, the allosaurus.

WILDLIFE
LIKE A LION IN ZION

Q. Which type of animal has more species in Zion National Park: reptiles or mammals?

A. Mammals. There are 76 species of mammals in Zion National Park, and 30 species of reptiles. Of the mammals, nearly half are rodents, including beavers and porcupines. Seventeen mammal species are bats. Larger mammals include mountain lions, bobcats, desert bighorn sheep, elk, mule deer, coyotes, foxes, and black bears. Of reptile species, 16 are lizards, 13 are snakes, and the other is the rare desert tortoise. Zion also has 7 species of amphibians—toads, frogs, and salamanders.

Q. When reggae music star Bob Marley wrote a hit song with the refrain "like a lion in Zion," he wasn't thinking of Zion National Park. But you might hear this song being played at a park ranger's evening program about mountain lions, which do live in Zion National Park. Wildlife biologists estimate that Zion holds between 10 and 30 mountain lions, but because mountain lions live in remote wilderness areas, it's hard to be sure of their numbers. Actually, the name "mountain lion" is only one of many names

given to the same species. How many different names does the mountain lion have?
1) 5   2) 12   3) 40
A. 3) 40. Other names include cougar, puma, and panther. According to the *Guinness Book of World Records*, the mountain lion has more names than any other species. Mountain lions are a widespread species, and people in different places gave them different names. If you lived in places without any mountains, you wouldn't think of a name like "mountain lion." Bryce Canyon too has mountain lions.

Q. How fast can mountain lions run?
1) 20 miles (32 km) per hour   2) 30 miles (48 km) per hour
3) 40 miles (64 km) per hour
A. 3) They've been clocked running at 40 miles (64 km) per hour.

Q. How far can mountain lions jump?
1) 10 feet (3 m)   2) 25 feet (7.6 m)   3) 40 feet (12 m)
A. 3) 40 feet (12 m). That's the length of a bus. And mountain lions can jump upward 18

Mountain lion exhibit

feet (5.5 m). That's nearly two stories. When you live among big cliffs, jumping is an important ability.

Q. What do mountain lions eat?
A. At Zion and Bryce Canyon, 90 percent of their prey is deer. Elsewhere in the Southwest, where there are more desert bighorn sheep, mountain lions rely more on bighorns. A mountain lion may go for a week between making kills, but then it can eat 30 pounds (13 kg) in one sitting. To find enough to eat, a mountain lion may range over hundreds of square miles. Mountain lions have never killed a human at Zion or Bryce Canyon. In the entire United States for the forty years between 1970 and 2010, mountain lions killed 17 humans. By comparison, approximately 40 Americans die of bee stings every year. One park ranger worked at Bryce Canyon for 19 years before she even glimpsed a mountain lion.

Wolves were last seen at Zion in 1936; grizzlies were last seen at Bryce Canyon in 1916.

Q. A century ago, Americans viewed predators like mountain lions and wolves as part of a wilderness that needed to be conquered. When Teddy Roosevelt traveled to the North Rim of the Grand Canyon to hunt mountain lions, he met game warden Jim Owens, who considered it part of his duty to kill mountain lions. In his career, how many mountain lions did Jim Owens kill?
1) 130   2) 330   3) 730

A. 3) 730. Of these, 130 were in southern Utah. In the 20th century, Americans killed an estimated 60,000 mountain lions. Early park rangers shared this hostility toward mountain lions. In 1929 the superintendent of Zion National Park declared: "The cougar is a killer...he is a wanton destroyer of living things. He... should be punished, and death is the only penalty possible for the cougar." Later, wildlife biologists recognized that predators are an essential part of a natural, balanced ecosystem. At Zion, the killing of mountain lions led to a population explosion of deer, and rangers had to trap deer and release them away from the park.

Q. Biologists estimate that North America once held as many as two million bighorn sheep. In the Southwest these were desert bighorn sheep, which are especially adapted to dry, rocky condi-tions. When Spanish explorers Domin-guez and Escalante came through Utah in 1776, they found that bighorn sheep occurred "in such abundance that the tracks look like those of great droves of tame sheep." But by 1960, the bighorn population had fallen dramatically. How many were left?

1) 18,000   2) 50,000   3) 200,000

A. 1) 18,000. Of these, about 7,000 were desert bighorn sheep. The bighorn sheep population dwindled due to hunting, loss of habitat, and diseases caught from domestic sheep. In the last 50 years, conservation efforts have boosted the total of desert bighorn sheep to more than 25,000. National parks have played an important role in this recovery effort. By the 1950s, desert bighorn sheep had disappeared from Zion National Park. Twenty years later, 30 sheep were reintroduced there in a pioneering experiment, and today the Zion population is about 200.

*Desert bighorn sheep were depicted in
Native American rock art in Zion.*

Q. Do bears live at Zion and Bryce Canyon?
A. Bears are very rare, and most of them are just migrating through the parks. Bears require lots of vegetation, such as berries, and the dry conditions at both Zion and Bryce Canyon aren't very appealing compared with wetter forests in the region. For a while, a black bear was hanging out at Bryce Canyon's Rainbow Point and raiding garbage cans.

Q. If you find a large animal track in the dirt and it has claw marks, which of these animals made it: a coyote, a mountain lion, or a bobcat?
A. A coyote. Like dogs, coyotes cannot retract their claws, so they leave claw marks. Like house cats, mountain lions and bobcats leave no claw marks. Coyote tracks are a bit more than two inches (5 cm) long, about half the length of a mountain lion track.

Q. Both Zion and Bryce Canyon have the gray fox. The gray fox has a unique ability. What?
1) It has no sense of smell, allowing it to hunt skunks.
2) It climbs trees.   3) It curls up to disguise itself as a gray rock.
A. 2) The gray fox is the only member of the dog family that can climb trees. This allows it to escape predators, and to feast
on juniper berries, which make up a large part of its diet. On Zion trails you'll often see gray fox scat, full of blue juniper berries.

Q. The deer you see at Zion and Bryce Canyon are mule deer. How did the mule deer get this name?
1) It is very stubborn.   2) Its ears are shaped like mule ears.
3) It is as tough as a mule.
A. 2) Its ears are shaped like mule ears. Mule deer are closely related to white-tailed deer but are found only in the western United States, especially in the Southwest. Male mule deer weigh up to 250 pounds (113 kg).

Q. Why are the beavers in Zion Canyon called "bank beavers"?
1) They store food in special food banks.

The horn-knocking of desert bighorn sheep can be heard a mile away.

2) They live in burrows in the river banks.

3) As they swim, they zigzag in "bank shots."

A. 2) They live in dens in the river banks. Bank beavers are the same species as the beavers that build dams, lakes, and lodges in rivers, but Zion's beavers learned long ago that the Virgin River is too swift and flood-prone to allow dams. Zion's beavers do gnaw on trees for food, as you can see all along the river. Beavers can swim half a mile (0.8 km) underwater, without coming up for air.

Q. How far can a skunk aim its spray accurately?

1) Five feet (1.5 m)   2) 10 feet (3 m)   3) 15 feet (4.5 m)

A. 3) 15 feet (4.5 m). The skunk's stinky spray is enough to keep most animals away, but not the great horned owl, which is the main predator of skunks. The great horned owl has a poor sense of smell.

Q. What's the most dangerous animal at Zion and Bryce Canyon?

1) Mountain lions   2) Squirrels   3) Rattlesnakes

A. 2) Squirrels. When tourists feed the squirrels, they often get bitten by mistake. Squirrels can carry diseases, so bite victims may require medical care. Feeding animals isn't good for the animals either. Most tourists give junk food, which is unhealthy for the animals, and when tourists are gone in winter, the animals may starve to death. There are good reasons why it's illegal to feed the animals in any national park. By the way, the golden-mantled ground squirrel is often mistaken for a chipmunk, since it is relatively small and doesn't have the long bushy tail of most squirrels. A chipmunk has a white stripe across its face, while the golden-mantled ground squirrel doesn't.

golden-mantled ground squirrel

chipmunk

Q. Springtime visitors to Zion, especially around the Emerald Pools, sometimes report hearing the baahing of sheep. What are they really hearing?

1) Bighorn sheep   2) Frogs   3) Ravens

A. 2) Tree frogs, which make an amazingly loud noise for such

Bighorn horns are hollow, while deer and elk antlers are solid.

a small animal. They are called tree frogs because they belong to a group of frogs with strong suction cups for climbing things, and they often climb up tree trunks. But in the Southwest, where there aren't so many trees, they will climb up rock faces. Their loud noise is their mating call.

Q. Zion Canyon is the only place in the world where you find the Zion snail. True or false: the Zion snail is the smallest snail in the world.
A. True. The Zion snail is so small, visitors walk right past it without seeing it. It is a pinhead-sized black speck that clings to the moist cliffs on the Riverside Walk. To avoid being swept away by flash floods, the Zion snail has a streamlined shell and a big "foot" for clinging to rocks.

Q. Does the Virgin River have any fish?
A. The river has four species of native fish, including the speckled dace and flannel mouth sucker. Trout sometimes escape from Kolob Reservoir and get into the Virgin River, but trout prefer clear and cold water, and the Virgin River inside Zion National Park is too turbid and warm for them.

Q. Zion's 16 species of lizards have some unique talents. The desert horned lizard, often called the horned toad or horny toad, can shoot blood from its eye to discourage predators. The blood has a skunky odor. How far can the lizard shoot its blood?
1) One foot (0.3 m)   2) Three feet (1 m)   3) Six feet (2 m)

Chuckwalla

A. 3) Six feet (2 m). Other lizard talents: the zebra-tailed lizard can stand on its hind legs and run 18 miles (29 km) per hour. The gecko stores so much fat in its tail, it can stay underground for months. The Gila monster is America's only venomous lizard. The chuckwalla escapes predators by crawling into narrow crevices in rocks and inflating its stomach to wedge itself in; Native

Beavers weigh up to 90 pounds (41 kg), and can fell an 8-inch (20 cm) diameter tree in 3 minutes.

Americans used sharp sticks to puncture the chuckwalla's stomach and pull them out of the rocks.

Q. What kinds of venomous creatures live at Zion and Bryce Canyon?
A. Both Zion and Bryce Canyon have the Western rattlesnake. The snakes you are most likely to see, like kingsnakes and gopher-snakes, are quite harmless. Even rattlesnakes aren't as aggressive as western movies portray them: they are usually eager to get away from people. Many of the people bitten by rattlesnakes are young males trying to show off their bravery. Zion, with its hotter deserts, has more venomous critters. Scorpions hang out in the crevices of rocks or trees and come out at night. Scorpion bites are almost never fatal: scorpion venom is made to kill insects or mice, not large animals. Tarantulas owe their bad reputation to Hollywood: they may be big, but their bite isn't dangerous. You aren't likely to see Gila monsters, which live only in the hottest

Rattlesnake

deserts and stay underground until evening.

Q. How many times per second does a rattlesnake shake its rattle?
1) Twice per second   2) 20 times   3) 90 times
A. 3) 90 times. The rattlesnake's rattle has one of the fastest muscle actions of any vertebrate in the world. It's as fast as the wing beats of hummingbirds.

Q. What do Zion shuttle bus drivers do when they come upon a snake lying in the road?
1) Run it over.
2) They get out, pick up the snake, and move it off the road.
3) Honk and wait for it to move.
A. 2) They move the snake. Fortunately, the long, hooked handle that drivers use for opening and closing the roof windows on the shuttle bus is a lot like the tools biologists use to move snakes. In a national park, it's not cool to run over the wildlife.

Skunks eat bees and wasps by the dozens,
ignoring being stung in the mouth.

Q. Of the 17 species of bats in Zion National Park, the one you are most likely to see—since it's the first to come out in the evening—is the western pipistrelle. How much does this bat weigh?
1) ¼ ounce (7 grams)   2) Two ounces (56 grams)
3) One pound (454 grams)
A. 1) Only ¼ ounce (7 grams). The western pipistrelle is the smallest bat in the United States. It is three inches (7 cm) long.

Q. How many species of birds are found in Zion National Park?
A. About 290—and counting. Dedicated bird watchers continue spotting new bird species. Some of these birds are just migrating through the area. Many more live in Zion seasonally. Year-round and common species include red-tailed hawks, Cooper's hawks, American kestrels, ravens, Steller's jays, wild turkeys, American dippers, and various songbirds.

Q. True or false: Zion has a songbird that flies underwater.
A. True. It's called the dipper, or water ouzel. It's the only songbird in America that spends most of its time in water. It can swim underwater for 30 seconds, as deep as 20 feet (6 m). Unlike waterfowl, which use webbed feet for swimming, the dipper uses its short wings. It also has strong legs and toes for walking in swift water. The dipper eats insects, larvae, and small fish. Look for it along the Virgin River and at the Emerald Pools. Sometimes it builds nests behind waterfalls and flies right through the falls. They are called dippers because they make frequent dipping motions. Biologists believe that these dipping motions are a form of communication with other birds. When a bird lives in rushing water, normal bird calls are difficult to hear.

Q. Wild turkeys are a common sight in Zion Canyon. If Benjamin Franklin had his way, turkeys and not bald eagles would have been the national symbol of the United States. Turkeys are natives of North America. In the Southwest, Native Americans domesticated

---

The Bryce Canyon mouse is a fossil mouse from the age of dinosaurs, discovered recently inside the park.

them for food, and used their feathers in clothes. For American pioneers, turkeys were such an important food source that they became symbols of national abundance, the center of Thanksgiving. Where do wild turkeys roost at night?
1) In thick grass   2) In trees   3) Underground
A. 2) In trees. Though wild turkeys may weigh 20 pounds (9 kg), they do indeed fly. But they are not the most dynamic flyers, and they know it. Just up the road from Zion Lodge there's a large area of cottonwood trees where turkeys roost at night. There's also a large hill that overlooks these trees. Turkeys will walk up this hill, launch themselves from it, and glide into the trees. They'd rather walk up a hill than fly up into a tree.

Q. Zion and Bryce Canyon have peregrine falcons. How fast can peregrines fly?
1) 100 miles (161 km) per hour   2) 200 miles (322 km) per hour
3) 300 miles (483 km) per hour
A. 2) Up to 200 miles (322 km) per hour in a dive. The peregrine falcon is the fastest animal on Earth. When they dive on another bird in flight, they seldom miss. This speed also helps peregrines migrate 15,000 miles (24,135 km) in one year.

Q. In the 1950s and 1960s, widespread use of the pesticide DDT was causing populations of raptors like peregrine falcons and bald eagles to plummet. Biologists estimate that when the United States was founded in 1776, the future 48 contiguous states held as many as half a million bald eagles, but in less than two centuries, there were only 400 nesting pairs of bald eagles left. There were only 39 nesting pairs of peregrine falcons. Some of those peregrines were in Zion Canyon. Why did Zion Canyon's

peregrine falcons do better than the ones elsewhere?
A. Zion is a long way from major agricultural areas, so its falcons weren't absorbing so much DDT. For the peregrines, as for Mormon pioneers, Zion was a sanctuary. Today, the total peregrine population is over 3,000. Bald eagles migrate to the Zion area in winter.

Of 33 species of raptors in Utah, 28 are found in Zion National Park.

Q. Another rare bird you could see in Zion is the California condor. They have the longest wingspan of any bird in North America. How long?
1) 6 feet (1.8 m)   2) 7.5 feet (2.2 m)   3) 9.5 feet (2.9 m)
A. 3) 9.5 feet (2.9 m). By contrast, the American bald eagle's wingspan is 8 feet (2.4 m). California condors can fly up to 100 miles (161 km) per day, and as high as three miles (4.8 km).

Q. Condors have heads and necks without any feathers. This is because of what they eat. What do condors eat?
A. Carrion—dead things. Condor beaks and talons aren't designed for hunting; condors have to find food that is already dead. Condor heads and necks are bare of feathers because condors stick their heads into dead bodies, and feathers would get messy with flesh, blood, and bugs. Because carrion can be hard to find, condors have to eat as much as possible when they can. They can eat three pounds (1.3 kg) of meat at one sitting, or about 15 percent of their own body weight. Condors can go for two weeks without eating.

Condors with tracking numbers on their wings

Q. Like bald eagles and peregrine falcons, the population of California condors was in serious decline. By 1982, how many California condors were left in the world?
1) 22   2) 222   3) 2,222
A. 1) Only 22. Biologists feared they would soon be extinct. In 1982 the remaining condors were removed from the wild and entered into a captive breeding program. Within five years, their population had risen to 63, and some condors were released to the wild in California. In 1996, six condors were released at the Vermilion Cliffs, in between the Grand Canyon and Zion, and dozens have been released there since then. As of 2010, the total population was up to 373, with 74 of those in Arizona and Utah. The condors soon took a liking to the Grand Canyon and began nesting there. It took them longer to discover Zion, but today in summer you have a good chance of seeing them soaring over Zion Canyon. Zion park rangers have counted as

The Interstate 15 corridor, just west of Zion,
is a major bird migration route.

many as 42 condors gathered in one place—at Lava Point, which is close to grazing areas, outside the park, that have dead sheep.

Q. Another carrion eater you may see at Zion and Bryce Canyon is the turkey vulture. True or false: turkey vultures got their name because they eat mostly wild turkeys.
A. False. Turkey vultures got their name because they look a lot like turkeys in size, brown color, and their bare, red head. Turkey vultures are only half the size of California condors, but when they are soaring high above you, this size difference can be hard to recognize. One way to tell them apart is that the turkey vulture flies with its wings canted upward in a "V" shape and often pivots from side to side, while a condor keeps its wings spread flat. Easiest of all, condors have radio transmitters and numbers on their wings.

Q. Another rare and endangered bird that lives in Zion National Park is the Mexican spotted owl. As of 1994 there were only 2,106 known Mexican spotted owls in the world. As of 2010, Zion National Park had 23 nesting pairs. In 2007, 27 chicks were born there. Mexican spotted owls usually live in forests, but in Zion they prefer somewhere else, somewhere even cooler and shadier than forests. Where is this?
A. Slot canyons, including Refrigerator Canyon on the Angels Landing Trail.

A Mexican spotted owl naps by day.

Q. Zion National Park has nine species of hummingbirds, and Bryce Canyon has four. Propelled by hearts that beat 250 times per minute, hummingbirds can fly 30 miles (48 km) per hour, which helps them migrate to Mexico in winter. They have 1,000 tiny feathers. They can fly backward, or hover in one spot to feed on flowers. How many flowers do they visit in one day?
1) 100   2) 250   3) 3,000
A. 3) Up to 3,000. Hummingbirds eat twice their weight in food every day. This would be like an adult human eating 350 pounds (158 kg) of food.

"Peregrine" is the Latin word for "wanderer."

Q. At both Zion and Bryce Canyon there are birds that zip around fast and make a swishing sound. What are they?

A. Swifts and swallows, which dive and curve swiftly in pursuit of flying insects. Both have dark wings and white bellies, but the white-throated swift's wings are longer and more pointed, while the violet-green swallow has a green back. As fast as swifts and swallows fly, peregrine falcons easily catch them in flight.

Violet-green swallow

Q. How many species of birds are found at Bryce Canyon National Park?

A. 210 species have been identified inside the park or within a few miles of it. As of 2010, there were four nesting pairs of peregrine falcons at Bryce Canyon, and all of them were nesting close to popular overlooks. But Bryce Canyon is too cold for condors, so they are rarely seen.

Q. How many species of mammals are found at Bryce Canyon National Park?

A. 73 species, about the same number as at Zion. Because Bryce Canyon has more wide-open grasslands than Zion, you have a better chance of seeing pronghorn. Bryce Canyon's elk are more elusive. The main road at Bryce Canyon goes right past prairie-dog towns. Bryce Canyon has 16 species of bats.

Q. How many species of reptiles are found at Bryce Canyon National Park?

A. 13. This is about half the number at Zion, which has more deserts. Bryce Canyon's reptiles include the Western rattlesnake and several other snakes, plus several lizards. Bryce Canyon also has four amphibians.

Q. What do these three animals have in common: pronghorn antelope, ringtail cats, and horned toads?
1) They were all described by the Lewis and Clark Expedition.
2) They are found only in Utah.

At Zion's Big Bend, a peregrine nest was used almost continuously since the 1930s.

3) Their names are wrong: the prong-horn isn't an antelope, the ringtail isn't a cat, and the horned toad isn't a toad. A. 3) All three names are wrong. The only true antelopes live in Africa. Ring-tails are related to raccoons, not cats. Horned toads are really lizards. Park rangers use the names "pronghorn," "ringtails," and "horned lizards."

Ringtail

Q. Pronghorn are named for their pronged horns. In the animal world there are two kinds of head armor: horns and antlers. Horns (as on bison and cattle) are made of keratin, or compressed hair, and are never shed. Antlers (as on deer) are made of bone and are shed and regrown every year. Pronghorn are unique: their horns have a permanent bony core, and then they grow longer keratin

horns that are shed every year. Pronghorn are also unique in how fast they run. How fast? 1) 40 miles (64 km) per hour   2) 50 miles (80 km) per hour 3) 60 miles (96 km) per hour A. 3) 60 miles (96 kg) per hour. At an age of three *days*, a pronghorn can outrun a hu-man. Of all the animals on Earth, only the cheetah can run faster than the pronghorn. Pronghorn needed to run this fast because America once had its own species of cheetah. When the American cheetah died out at the end of the Ice Age, it left no predator fast enough to catch pronghorn, so the prong-horn population increased to an estimated 40 million by the time Europeans arrived in America. There were as many pronghorn as there were bison. By 1900, overhunting had reduced the pronghorn population to about 20,000. In Utah, pronghorn disappeared completely, but they were reintroduced in the 1970s.

Q. A century ago, the western United States held an estimated five *billion* prairie dogs. Prairie dogs aren't really dogs, but rodents.

Zion's hummingbird nests include cottonwood seeds and spider webs.

They are highly sociable, building large colonies. Due to disease and elimination by ranchers, prairie dog populations have plummeted. Bryce Canyon National Park holds one of five species of prairie dogs in the American West, the Utah prairie dog. By what percent has the total population of the Utah prairie dog dropped?
1) 50 percent   2) 72 percent
3) 98 percent

A. 3) 98 percent. In territory, their habitat has dwindled from 448,000 acres (181,300 hc) to only 7,000 acres (2,839 hc). By 1950, the Utah prairie dog was extinct in Bryce Canyon National Park, but it was reintroduced. To spot a prairie dog town, just look for the "Prairie Dog Crossing" sign on the main road. Prairie dogs dig tunnels up to ten feet (3 m) deep, and hibernate in winter.

Long-tailed weasel in summer (left) and winter.

Q. Bryce Canyon's long-tailed weasel is strong enough to tackle prey twice its own size. In summer the weasel is colored brown. What color does it turn in winter?
A. White, to blend in with the snow.

Q. Most birds flee Bryce Canyon's long winters for warmer places. But the dusky grouse stays at Bryce Canyon all year. What do they eat in wintertime?
1) The needles and buds of spruce and fir trees
2) Nuts they gathered and stored
3) The droppings of long-tailed weasels
A. 1) The needles and buds of spruce and fir trees

Q. Another bird that stays all winter at Bryce Canyon is the raven. Biologists have proven that ravens are one of the smart-

---

In relative size, hummingbird eggs are equal to human mothers giving birth to 25-pound (11 kg) babies.

est of birds. One Bryce Canyon pair of ravens figured out how to raid bear-resistant garbage cans: one raven held open the heavy lid while the other raven went inside. Raven intelligence helps ravens survive in the toughest environments, from deserts to the arctic. Ravens are related to crows, but they are larger, as large as hawks, and have stronger beaks. Crows prefer agricultural areas, which is why you see scarecrows and not scareravens. Ravens thrive in the wilderness. Sometimes when people see ravens in hot deserts, they wonder why ravens are black—isn't black the worst color for the desert? But when you see ravens at Bryce Canyon, the answer is more obvious. Why are ravens black?

A. Black helps them absorb sunlight in the winter and stay warm. Ravens are primarily a northern bird, surviving in cold that would kill off most birds. For agricultural peoples, ravens and crows are seen as evil birds, since they eat

Raven (left) and crow tails in flight.

crops. It was this view of ravens that Edgar Allan Poe repeated in his famous poem, "The Raven." But to northern peoples, such as Inuits and Vikings, who relied more on hunting and fishing, the raven didn't represent any competition for food, and the raven is seen as a wise and benevolent god. For many people who love the Southwest and love the sight of ravens soaring joyfully through canyons, ravens are a favorite bird, an icon of canyon country.

One of the greatest threats to condors is lead poisoning, from eating lead bullets in dead game.

A desert tortoise can go for a year without drinking water.

PLANTS
TREES AS BEAUTIFUL AND STRANGE AS THE ROCKS

Juniper

Q. At 232 square miles (601 sq km), Zion National Park makes up about 0.18 percent of the Colorado Plateau. Of all the plant species found on the Colorado Plateau, what percent of them are found in Zion National Park?
1) 0.18 percent   2) 10 percent   3) 60 percent
A. 3) About 60 percent. With its wide range of elevations and plant habitats, Zion National Park is a microcosm of the Colorado Plateau. Zion National Park makes up about 3 percent of the area of Utah, but it has 28 percent of the plant species found in Utah.

Q. How many plant species are found in Zion National Park?
A. Biologists have identified over 900 species of plants, but since Zion has lots of still-unstudied areas, with lots of diverse habitants, biologists are confident there must be well over 1,000 species.

Q. What are the big trees in Zion Canyon?
A. Cottonwood trees, or more specifically, a subspecies called the Fremont cottonwood, named for explorer John C. Fremont. The cottonwood is unique to North America, and got its name from the

cotton-like parachutes on which its seeds ride the wind. Fremont cottonwoods are found in the American Southwest, where their shade is especially appreciated. Pioneers loved to see cottonwoods because they signaled the presence of reliable, flowing water. In autumn, cottonwood leaves turn brilliant gold. Artists like Georgia O'Keefe and Maynard Dixon loved cottonwoods and painted them often. As a boy, Walt Disney loved to sit beneath a giant backyard cottonwood, which he called his "dreaming tree," and he imagined that trees, mice, and deer were his magical friends.

Fremont cottonwoods

Q. The cottonwood tree in front of Zion Lodge seems especially big. Why is this? And how old is this tree?
A. The tree on the front lawn of Zion Lodge is larger than most cottonwoods because the lawn gets plenty of watering, and the tree has no competition from other trees. Cottonwoods are very thirsty trees: the Zion Lodge tree is estimated to drink 1,000 gallons (3,785 liters) of water every day. This tree was probably planted in 1929. One 1929 photograph of Zion Lodge shows no trees on the lawn, but other photos from 1929 show newly planted trees. Today's tree was first documented in 1934, on a topographical map. Generations of Zion visitors have fond memories of picnicking under this tree.

Q. How many seeds can a Fremont cottonwood tree produce in one year?
1) 10,000   2) 100,000   3) 48 million
A. 3) The highest estimate is 48 million. An Eastern cottonwood, which grows in the eastern United States, produces "only" 25 million seeds. Like most desert plants, the Fremont cottonwood needs to produce lots of seeds to make sure that a few find a spot with good soil and water. With help from the wind, cottonwood seeds may travel for miles.

John C. Fremont, of the Fremont cottonwood, was the first Republican candidate for president, in 1856.

Q. Often, environmental problems arise when humans make changes without realizing all the consequences. This is what happened in Zion Canyon in the 1930s, when rock revetments were built along the Virgin River to stop it from flooding or changing course. But the revetments also stopped new cottonwood trees from sprouting. Why did preventing floods also prevent new cottonwood trees?

A. To germinate, cottonwood seeds require moist soil, which is provided by springtime floods. Without floods, very few new cottonwoods have been starting out. As older cottonwoods die off, the floor of Zion Canyon is being left bare of cottonwoods.

Q. In the springtime, many cottonwood trees in Zion hold little white "tents." What are these?

A. These are webs woven by a caterpillar. The webs look so much like little tents that the caterpillar is called the "tent caterpillar." They devour the leaves of cottonwood trees, but fortunately cottonwoods can generate a new set of leaves. Then the tent caterpillars drop from the trees onto rocks, shrubs, buildings, or cars, weave little white cocoons, and turn into moths. Unlike gypsy moths in the eastern U.S., which are an invasive species, Zion's moths are longtime natives.

As you travel around Zion, Bryce Canyon, and the rest of the Colorado Plateau, you'll see the types of trees and other plants changing from area to area. The main secret of plant distribution comes down to one word: elevation.

With every 1,000 feet (305 m) you gain, temperatures cool off by about 4 F, and there is more precipitation. Most trees and other plants can grow only within a specific range of temperatures and precipitation. You can see this at both Zion and Bryce Canyon. As you stand in Zion Canyon at about 4,000 feet (1,219 m) in elevation, you are surrounded by cottonwoods, but as you look up 2,500 feet (762 m) to the rim, you are seeing ponderosa pines (which grow tall and straight, and the older ones are cinnamon colored).

As you enter Bryce Canyon National Park you are at about 8,000 feet (2,438 m) and surrounded by ponderosa pines, but as you drive the Scenic Drive to Rainbow Point, which is at

---

Due to aggressive control efforts, Zion Canyon has few tamarisks, a big invasive tree problem elsewhere.

9,115 feet (2,778 m), the ponderosas disappear and you are surrounded by white fir, blue spruce, Douglas-fir, and aspen trees. These trees are typical of what you'd find in Canada; by gaining 1,000 feet (305 m) in elevation, it's like traveling hundreds of miles north to a different climate.

In between the elevations of Zion Canyon and Bryce Canyon, you'll see pinyon-juniper forests, often called the "pygmy forest" because both pinyon and juniper trees are relatively short. Pinyons reach about 30 feet (9 m) tall, junipers only 20 feet (6 m). Both trees have a twisted look, but you can tell them apart because pinyons have needles (or "pins"), while juniper leaves are more scale-like. Pinyon trees are famous for their "pine nuts," while juniper trees have berries. Juniper bark peels off in string-like pieces. Pinyon-juniper forests are found between about 4,000 and 7,000 feet (1,219 m-2,133 m) which includes most of the Colorado Plateau.

Q. While many trees depend on the wind to spread their seeds, the pinyon tree depends on one bird, the pinyon jay. A pinyon jay can carry 50 pinyon seeds in its mouth at once. A pair of pinyon jays can cache 13,000 seeds per year. Pinyon jays have incredible memories, allowing them to find most of their caches. The trees, of course, are counting on the pinyon jays to forget some seeds. Pinyon seeds, or nuts, are an incredibly rich source of nutrition. Which has more calories: a pound of pinyon nuts, or a pound of Hershey's chocolate?

Pinyon jay harvesting pine nuts

A. A pound of pinyon nuts has 2,800 calories, and a pound of Hershey's chocolate has 2,460 calories. Because of their seed caches, pinyon jays can begin breeding earlier in the year than most birds, which have to wait for spring to create a food supply.

Riparian zones (lush vegetation zones along rivers) make up only one percent of the Southwest.

Joke: If you see two pinyon trees on one side of the road and one pinyon tree on the other side, what does this mean? Answer: It's a difference of a pinyon.

Q. As you travel around the Zion and Bryce Canyon region, you see large zones of dead trees, and it doesn't look like they were killed by fire. What killed them?

A. The bark beetle, which is plaguing forests throughout the American West. Bark beetles are a normal part of forest ecology, but usually they attack only old and sick trees.

Younger, healthy trees can produce enough sap to seal off their bark against the beetles. But in long, severe droughts, trees can't make enough sap to defend themselves against bark beetles. Bark beetles are killing forests that have survived for many centuries; this could be another symptom of global climate change. Normally, bark beetles are killed off by long cold spells, but with milder winters in the Southwest, more bark beetles are surviving. Bark beetle-killed trees also greatly increase the risk of forest fires.

Q. The National Park Service, which is supposed to preserve nature, now often lets forest fires burn, or even sets its own "prescribed fires." Why is this?

Prescribed burn of downed timber in Zion National Park.

A. For most of the 20th century, the National Park Service thought of forest fires as an enemy. Fires were predators that destroyed trees, just like mountain lions destroyed deer. But just as predators are a necessary part of a balanced ecosystem, fire too is

Zion's worst forest fire burned 10,516 acres (4,255 hc) in 2006. Bryce Canyon's worst fire burned 1,942 acres (786 hc) in 2009.

a normal part of the forest ecosystem. In normal ponderosa and pinyon-juniper forests, lightning starts a low-intensity ground fire every few years, and the ground fire burns up all the dry needles, fallen limbs, and young trees on the forest floor but does little harm to mature trees. Ponderosas have thick bark and elevated branches that resist ground fires. But if humans suppress forest fires, the ground litter builds up for decades, until they fuel massive wildfires that can kill whole forests. Today, the National Park Service may allow lightning-caused fires to run their natural course, as long as they meet management objectives and remain within certain safety limits.

Q. The largest flower in southern Utah is the sacred datura, or angels-trumpet. The trumpet-shaped flowers are white, and

This horse is dangerously close to sacred datura blossoms.

about six inches (15 cm) wide. But the sacred datura is dangerous. Why? A. It contains a potent neurotoxin that can cause blindness, seizures, and even death. It is also called Jimson weed, and can cause horses to go crazy. It is called sacred datura because Native Americans used it in religious ceremonies. Native Americans knew how to prepare it carefully, but even they sometimes died from it.

Q. When do wildflowers bloom at Zion and Bryce Canyon? A. At Zion, wildflowers bloom from March to October. A majority of flowers bloom in the spring, but summer bloomers include favorites like columbines, and about 20 flowers bloom in the fall. In Bryce Canyon's much cooler climate the wildflower season is only half as long; the peak is in late June and early July.

Q. How did the plant "scouring rush" get its name?
1) You have to scour the land to find one.
2) Pioneers used it to scour dirty pots and pans.
3) The plant has a sour taste, and one pioneer misspelled "souring."

White is a common color for flowers that bloom at night.

A. 2) The plant stems are so high in silica that they are rough, and good for scrubbing pots and pans. Of course, in a dry climate, a marsh plant like a rush isn't common. But as you walk up Zion's Riverside Walk you'll come across a little marsh. The seeds of these plants probably got there by being washed down the Virgin River, or were carried by birds.

Q. "Resurrection moss" is a moss that usually looks dry, brown, and crusty. In fact, you could easily think it was dead. But when rains fall on resurrection moss, what happens to it in about one minute?
A. It turns deep green, and takes on more form and texture. Like many desert plants, the resurrection moss has to endure long dry periods, and when rain comes, it responds quickly to take advantage of it.

Q. What's the plant with the long, thick, bayonet-like leaves that point upward?
A. The yucca, which you might think is a cactus for its sharp points, but it actually belongs to the agave family. The edges of the leaves have fibers curling off them. These fibers are so strong that Native Americans used them to make ropes, baskets, sandals (see page 66), and mats, yet the fibers are so slender they were used to paint thin lines on pottery.

Q. Zion has several types of cactus, including prickly pear, cholla, and hedgehog cactus. Cacti are masters of water conservation. The average American uses 140 gallons (529 liters) of water every day. How long could a cactus last on 140 gallons?
1) 6 months   2) 5 years   3) 50 years
A. 3) 50 years. Cacti are so sensitive to water supply that in a dry year they will skip producing flowers and seeds. Yet after a wet winter and spring, Zion is full of red, yellow, and pink cactus flowers.

The Zion daisy grows only in and near Zion Canyon.

Q. Cowboys and environmentalists don't always see eye-to-eye on how to manage the land. But when both cowboys and environmentalists see the grasses that fill Zion Canyon, both of them frown. Why is this?

A. The dominant grass on the floor of Zion Canyon is cheatgrass, or drooping brome. It is a highly invasive weed. In America cheatgrass first appeared in New York in 1861, and by 1928 it had swept across the whole country. It easily outcompetes native grasses, taking over rangelands and pastures, and its sharp barbs make it impossible for livestock to eat it. Cheatgrass also makes a much more explosive fuel for wildfires. If you've walked through the grasses at Zion and ended up with lots of sharp seeds stuck in your socks and shoes, it was probably cheatgrass.

Q. The invasive plants at Zion and Bryce Canyon and other national parks tend to be concentrated along the roads. Why is this?
1) Animals ate the plants farther from the roads.
2) The plants grew from seeds that arrived on cars.
3) Plants along roads get more water.

A. 2) Seeds "hitchhiked" on cars, stuck on radiator grills or in undercarriage mud.

Q. How many plant species live in Bryce Canyon National Park?
1) 400   2) 700   3) 1,000

A. 1) More than 400. This is less than half the number found in Zion National Park. Bryce Canyon's high elevation, harsh winters, and lack of water sources in summer give it fewer plant habitats than Zion.

Q. Manzanita is a shrub found at both Zion and Bryce Canyon. It has an odd-looking trunk, a twisting mixture of ordinary wood and what looks like dark red leather. While most plants  hold their leaves horizontally, like an outstretched hand, manzanitas hold their leaves vertically. This allows this evergreen plant to avoid having too much snow piling up on its leaves, and to avoid too much sun exposure in summer. One time a Bryce Canyon ranger, leading a nature walk, bet his crowd one dollar if they could find a horizontal manzanita leaf. Who won this bet?

The monkeyflower got its name because it looks like the face of a monkey.

A. The ranger, of course. It doesn't pay to bet against rangers in their own park.

Q. One of many odd sights at Bryce Canyon is the trees growing on the tops of hoodoos. These trees were probably planted by a bird named the Clark's nutcracker. One Clark's nutcracker can stash away 40,000 seeds in one year, and it remembers the location of 70 percent of those seeds. Who was the Clark's nutcracker named for?
1) William Clark, of the Lewis and Clark Expedition
2) Clark Kent, because the bird flies like Superman
3) Dick Clark, of *American Bandstand*, because the bird does a little dance
A. 1) William Clark, who scientifically described this bird on the Lewis and Clark Expedition.

Q. Another odd place for trees to grow is in the deep, narrow canyons among the Bryce Canyon hoodoos, such as in Wall Street. What are the big, tall trees there?
A. Douglas-fir trees. Biologists estimate they are up to 600 years old.

Q. On Bryce Canyon's Bristlecone Loop Trail you can see the type of tree that lives longer than any organism on Earth: the bristlecone pine. Bristlecone pines often have odd, twisted, gnarly shapes, which seem like the perfect match for Bryce Canyon's odd, twisted rock formations. Bristlecone pine trees grow only in the American West. How old is the oldest-known bristlecone pine tree?
1) 980 years   2) 2,120 years   3) 4,780 years
A. 3) 4,780 years. Trees can be dated by their tree rings, even while the trees are alive. This 4,780-year-old tree is in the White Mountains of California. It began growing at around the time the Egyptian pyramids were being built. The oldest-known bristlecone pine tree at

Bryce Canyon was 1,600 years old—it started growing at around the time the Roman Empire was ending. But this tree died recently.

The Virgin River holds watercress, one of about 100 plants introduced to Zion by pioneers.

Q. Bristlecone pines can survive in conditions where other trees can't: on rocky ledges, in poor soil, in heavy snow, in strong winds, and in severe droughts. What special ability allows bristlecone pines to survive droughts?
1) Very deep roots.   2) They can absorb water from the air.
3) They can shut down metabolism in many of their branches.
A. 3) They can temporarily shut down metabolism in some branches.

Q. To survive in very harsh conditions, bristlecone pines grow very slowly. As part of this slow-growth strategy, bristlecones retain their needles longer than other pine trees. Producing new needles takes lots of energy, nutrients, and water. Other pine trees replace their needles every 2-3 years. How long do bristlecones retain their needles?
1) 15 years   2) 40 years   3) 100 years
A. 2) Up to 40 years. Bristlecone pines also have unusually dense and highly resinous wood. While other trees are often damaged by insects, fungi, and bacteria, this almost never happens to bristlecone pines.

Q. Another odd tree found at Bryce Canyon is the limber pine.

How did it get the name "limber pine"?
1) It has lots of limbs.
2) Its limbs are very limber (flexible).
3) This was a misspelling of "lumber."
A. 2) Its limbs are so limber, you can tie them in a knot. Since limber pines grow at elevations where lots of snow piles up on branches, this flexibility prevents branches from breaking off.

The madder plant is so soft, pioneers used it to stuff mattresses and pillows.

HISTORY
NATIVE AMERICANS, PIONEERS, NATIONAL PARKS

Native-American-
made yucca sandal

Q. When did humans first arrive in the Zion and Bryce Canyon area?

A. At the end of the last Ice Age, about 12,000 years ago. These people survived by hunting large Ice Age animals, like mammoths. Archaeologists have found their spear points associated with mammoth bones. As Ice Age animals died out, people hunted smaller game, such as deer and desert bighorn sheep. At Bryce Canyon, archaeologists have found one projectile point that may be 10,000 years old. People also gathered wild nuts and fruits and vegetables. They knew all kinds of uses for wild plants, including as medicines. Since hunter-gatherers had to continue moving, they didn't build stone houses that might have left ruins for us to see today.

Q. But there are plenty of stone ruins in southern Utah. Who built these?

A. Hunting and gathering is a tough way to make a living, so humans were usually ready to give it up for agriculture, which allowed them to grow their own nutrition and stay in the same place. By around 2,000 years ago agriculture was being developed in the American Southwest, boosted by the arrival of corn, beans, and squash from Mexico, where these crops had been grown for a long time. Corn, beans, and squash provided a balanced diet and good crop rotation to maintain the soil. The people who developed agriculture in the Southwest are called the Ancestral Puebloans (also called Anasazi), the ancestors of today's pueblo tribes. Because they were staying in the same places for a whole lifetime, they began building solid stone houses, or pueblos. The center of Ancestral Puebloan society was the Four Corners area, with its large ceremonial centers such as Chaco Canyon and Mesa Verde. Southwestern Utah was on the fringe of the Ancestral Puebloan world, so the population there was thinner and the villages smaller.

Q. Are there any Ancestral Puebloan ruins in Zion and Bryce Canyon national parks?

A. Bryce Canyon's long winters and lack of water in summer made it an unappealing place for year-round dwellings. Since Zion had a milder climate and a lot more water, the Ancestral Puebloans built more villages there, but any Ancestral Puebloan structures on the floor of Zion Canyon got swept away by floods centuries ago. On cliffs and boulders, the Ancestral Puebloans left lots of rock art. In some places where the Ancestral Puebloans needed to travel up steep rock slopes, they carved steps into the stone. One such stone stairway goes up the slope above Weeping Rock, on the way to Echo Canyon. But it's not clear if these steps were carved by the Ancestral Puebloans, or the people who followed them, the Paiutes.

Q. Why did the Ancestral Puebloans disappear?

A. Around the year 1200 AD, a long, severe drought struck the Southwest. Farming in the desert was always a vulnerable way of life, and when the rains stopped for a few years, an agricultural society soon fell apart. But the Ancestral Puebloans didn't really disappear. They migrated to places with springs and rivers that still allowed agriculture, such as the Hopi mesas in Arizona or the

---

Archaeologists have found over 100 Native American projectile points at Bryce Canyon, many of them over 1,000 years old.

Rio Grande River in New Mexico. They became today's Puebloan peoples, who still continue many of their ancient ways of life.

Q. When the Ancestral Puebloans abandoned most of the Southwest, was the land left empty of people?
A. Not for long. The same drought that brought down Ancestral Puebloan society also made life very tough for the tribes that survived by hunting and gathering in the Great Basin and Mojave Desert to the west of Zion and Bryce Canyon. These peoples soon migrated to higher ground in search of more water, game, and plants. This is how the Southern Paiutes came to live in the Zion and Bryce Canyon area.

Q. How did the Southern Paiutes live?
A. They continued the hunting and gathering lifestyle they had practiced in the Great Basin and Mojave Desert. This was now the only lifestyle that could succeed where agriculture had failed. The Southern Paiutes lived in wikiups, domes made from the limbs of trees and bushes. They were masters of weaving baskets for holding and carrying everything, even water. In some places with reliable water and good soil, the Southern Paiutes developed agriculture. The Southern Paiutes still live in the Zion and Bryce Canyon region today. They left  their names in Zion Canyon, such as Sinawava, Mukuntuweap, and Pa'rus, and if you attend ranger programs at Bryce Canyon, you may hear Paiute stories about the hoodoos or the night sky.

Q. Who was the first Euro-American to see Zion Canyon?
A. Morman pioneer Nephi Johnson. Several famous exploring parties had come close to Zion Canyon, but missed it. In 1776 the Spanish padres Dominguez and Escalante came within 20 miles (32 km) of Zion Canyon, and they must have seen its cliffs in the distance, but they had no reason to go there, since they were searching for a route to California. Other near-misses were fur trappers Jedediah Smith in 1825 and Peg-Leg Smith in 1827, and explorer John C. Fremont in 1844. Nephi Johnson arrived in 1858, the first Euro-American known to have seen Zion Canyon, guided there by Paiutes. Before long,

In Zion Canyon, Native Americans gathered wild grapes, cattail roots, and wild strawberries.

American exploring expeditions were seeking out Zion, including John Wesley Powell in 1872, and geologist Grove Karl Gilbert of the Wheeler survey. Gilbert became the first Euro-American to explore the Narrows, riding his horse up it. He called it "the most wonderful defile it has been my good fortune to behold."

Q. Who were the first Euro-American settlers in the Zion and Bryce Canyon area?

A. Soon after the Mormons arrived in the Great Salt Lake Valley in 1847, they began systematically exploring and settling Utah and nearby states, founding hundreds of towns. Because the Mormons didn't have the long experience of Native Americans, the Mormons established some towns in the wrong places, where they were doomed by droughts or floods. But hundreds of these towns succeeded. Of the towns the Mormons built near Zion Canyon in the 1860s, Springdale and Rockville are still alive, while others, like Grafton, were abandoned. The Mormons established six towns just east of Bryce Canyon, three of which remain. Many of the original pioneer families in the Zion and Bryce Canyon area are still there today, and they've played leading roles in the development of the national parks and tourism.

Q. Who was the first Euro-American to live inside Zion Canyon?

A. While Mormon pioneers began arriving in the Zion area in  the early 1850s, it was six years before Nephi Johnson became the first Euro-American to enter Zion Canyon itself. Access to the inner half of Zion Canyon was made difficult by all the rock debris of the Sentinel slide. But the flat, green lands inside Zion Canyon were hard to resist. In 1863 Isaac Behunin—the man who named Zion Canyon—built

Nephi Johnson a cabin near today's Zion Lodge. Before moving west, Isaac Behunin had helped build the Erie Canal. The Behunin's crude cabin had only one room—for six children! There was lots of laundry too. To make a wash basin, Isaac cut down a cottonwood tree and dug a bowl into its stump.

Q. The Behunins had chickens, who were accustomed to going to bed at sunset. But when the Behunins moved the chickens into

---

The Paiutes made poisoned arrows from the venom of rattlesnakes, mixed with crushed black widow spiders.

Zion Canyon, the chickens became very confused about bedtime. Why was this?

A. In Zion Canyon, with its towering "horizon," the sun "set" a few hours before darkness actually fell. The chickens tried going to bed at "sunset," only to become restless when darkness didn't follow, and they came out of the coop again. Zion Canyon's limited sunlight also limited its value for farming. The Behunins soon left Zion. Isaac's son returned 57 years later, after Zion had become a national park, and he said the canyon hadn't changed at all.

Q. What kinds of crops did the Mormon pioneers grow in Zion Canyon?

A. Wheat, potatoes, sorghum, vegetables, and fruit trees including apples, pears, apricots, and plums. Some of these fruit trees are still alive today, scattered among the cottonwood trees in the park campgrounds. Some of the irrigation ditches in the campgrounds were built by the pioneers.

Q. The pioneers who settled in remote, rugged places like Zion needed lots of ingenuity. They also needed lots of lumber. The cottonwood trees in Zion Canyon were too brittle to make good lumber, but on the rim 2,500 feet (762 m) above there were ponderosa pines, which make great lumber. But now the pioneers faced the problem of how to get those trees down the cliffs. What did they do?
1) Tossed them over the cliffs.   2) Used giant parachutes.
3) Built a cable tramway.

A. 3) At first they tried tossing the trees over the cliffs, but when the trees hit bottom, they were smashed into splinters. To haul lumber around the cliffs on wagons would have taken two weeks. A 15-year-old boy, David Flanigan, had the idea of building a cable system, but it took years to convince others this was a good idea. From 1901 to 1926 the cable hauled many thousands of tons of lumber from a mill on the rim to the canyon floor near Weeping Rock. You can still see the wooden framework of the cable system perched atop the cliff, if you look up from Big Bend or the Weeping Rock shuttle stop.

When Zion became a national park, local residents were so proud, some named their sons "Park."

Q. How did they build such a long cable system?

A. It wasn't easy. When David and his helpers first hauled 40 pounds (18 kg) of bailing wire to the top of the cliff, they discovered that it wasn't nearly long enough to reach the ground, and they had to get more. As they

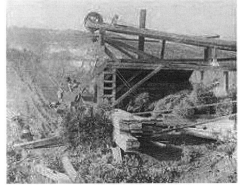

The cable works around 1900

lowered the wire, it got tangled in a tree limb. They got a rifle and shot off the tree limb. They took months to rig up the wires and a system of pulleys and brakes. The bailing wire proved too flimsy, so it was replaced by a strong cable. The cable and load were so heavy that they often caused the pulleys to overheat. Around 1912 lightning struck and burned the cliff-top wooden framework, and the cable fell to the canyon floor. But the cable works was rebuilt.

Q. Up to 45 men worked at the lumber mill at the top of the cable works. How did they get to and from work?
1) They rode the cable.   2) They hiked.   3) They parachuted down.
A. 1) They rode the cable. The ride took only two or three minutes. To test out the cable for passengers, David Flanigan put his dog Darkey into the cable basket and raised him to the top. Darkey arrived "real scart" and refused to go close to the cable again. But Darkey's heroism is still honored today in the name of the restaurant at Flanigan's Inn in Springdale: The Spotted Dog. A later owner of the cable works weighed 300 pounds (135 kg) and he rode up and down the cable frequently.

National Park Service interpreters are supposed to know their parks better than anyone, but few interpreters could match the qualifications of longtime Zion ranger J.L. Crawford. Crawford was born 200 yards (182 m) from the future Zion National Park Visitor Center (today's Human History

The last job of the Zion cable works was lowering logs to build Zion Lodge, which took 240,000 board feet of lumber.

Museum). Crawford's grandfather had pioneered this land in 1879. J.L. Crawford's father Louis was a pioneering Zion photographer, and his work included making postcards for tourists. J.L. Crawford was born five years before Zion became a national park. As a kid, Crawford helped the park's ranger-naturalist to collect lizards and insects. Later, working as a dishwasher at Zion Lodge, Crawford hurried to get done with work so he could attend ranger talks. In the 1930s Crawford worked for the Civilian Conservation Corps and helped build the stone pillar for the park entrance sign at Springdale. He became a ranger in 1946. He wrote lots of poetry about Zion and used it in his ranger programs. Crawford was interviewed in the Ken Burns PBS series *The National Parks*.

Q. What do these things have in common: the ice cream cone, the hot dog, and Zion Canyon?

A. They were all introduced to the American public at the 1904

St. Louis World's Fair. Millions of Americans got their first look at Zion through the paintings of Frederick Dellenbaugh at the fair. The public enthusiasm for Zion helped persuade President William Howard Taft to make Zion a national monument

St. Louis World's Fair

only five years later. When you are walking around Zion and eating ice cream cones and hot dogs, think of how these three things all belong together.

Q. When Frederick Dellenbaugh's paintings of Zion were on display at the 1904 St. Louis World's Fair, a youth named Avid Hirschi from the town of Rockville, just outside Zion, came upon them and was pleased to see how much interest they were stirring up. He was also surprised to hear the crowd expressing skepticism about whether the paintings depicted a real place, since their scenes seemed too wonderful to be true. What did Hirschi do to prove that Zion was real?

The first car arrived in Zion in 1912.

1) He got out a photograph.   2) He pointed at his shoelaces.
3) He swore it on a Bible.
A. 2) He pointed to his shoelaces, made from buckskin, and pointed to the spot in one painting where he had shot the deer from which he'd made these shoelaces. The crowd was impressed.

Q. Both Zion and Bryce Canyon became national monuments before they became national parks. What percent of America's national parks were originally national monuments?
1) 10 percent   2) 25 percent   3) 50 percent
A. 3) Nearly 50 percent. Of 58 national parks, 28 started as national monuments. A national monument can be created by a presidential proclamation, while a national park requires a vote of Congress.

Q. Zion became a national monument in 1909 and took ten years to become a national park. Bryce Canyon became a national monument in 1923 and took five years to become a national park. Compared with other national monuments that later became national parks, did Zion and Bryce Canyon take more years, or fewer years, to be promoted from a monument to a park?
A. Fewer years, by far. The average wait for a national monument to become a national park is 33 years. Many parks have waited over 60 years. Death Valley, Glacier Bay, and Saguaro each took 61 years; Denali took 63 years; Black Canyon of the Gunnison took 66 years; and Great Sand Dunes took 68 years. Only four parks, all in Alaska, took less time than Bryce Canyon to become parks. Only eight parks took less time than Zion. Even the Grand Canyon waited eleven years to be promoted from a monument to a park.

Q. If you rank the 58 national parks in the order they were created, where would Zion rank?
1) 3rd   2) 12th   3) 20th
A. 2) 12th. Zion became a national park in 1919, a few months after Grand Canyon became a national park. The year 1919 may have been the best-ever "graduating class" year for national parks. Other good years included 1890 (Yosemite and Sequoia), 1929 (Acadia and Grand Teton) and 1934 (Great Smoky Mountains and Everglades). Bryce Canyon was the 15th national park.

The first two bridges over the Virgin River at Zion's
Canyon Junction were swept away by flash floods.
Today's sturdy bridge opened in 1930.

Q. How many visitors came to Zion in its first full year as a national park (1920)?
1) 3,692   2) 55,692   3) 250,692
A. 1) Only 3,692. In Zion's first years as a national monument, only a few hundred people had visited it annually. Zion was remote

Union Pacific Railroad buses at Zion Lodge, 1929

and inaccessible, with the nearest train station nearly 100 miles (161 km) away in the town of Lund. In 1923 the Union Pacific Railroad built a spur line from Lund to Cedar City, still 50 miles (80 km) from Zion. The Union Pacific began bus tours to Zion, Bryce Canyon, Cedar Breaks, and the North Rim of the Grand Canyon. The bus tours were run by the brothers Chauncey and Gronway Parry, and cost $140 for an eight-day tour of all four parks. In Kanab, Utah, the Parrys built the Parry Lodge, which became a base for movie stars when the Kanab area became a major location for filming westerns. In 1930 Zion visitation was up to 55,000; in 1940, 165,000. It hit the one million mark in 1973, and the two million mark in 1990. In its first 100 years, Zion National Park had 86 million visitors.

The tour bus ride to Zion and Bryce Canyon was long, bumpy, hot, and dusty, so the tour drivers developed a lively sense of humor to keep passengers entertained. Here are some of the jokes they told:

"It's so dry here, the trees chase the dogs."

"Fourteen prospectors were killed last year when jackrabbits kicked them to death for their canteens."

"Lizards often take turns giving piggy-back rides to one another to keep their feet from getting too hot."

"This year the rattlesnakes are especially aggressive. In fact, a couple of weeks ago, one bit a driver. They rushed him to the hospital where he was worked on by four doctors, but it was no good, they couldn't save the rattlesnake."

Completion of the Zion-Mt. Carmel Highway shortened the distance from Zion to Bryce Canyon from 149 to 88 miles (239 to 141 km), and boosted visitation at Bryce Canyon by 63% the next year.

Q. In 1917, Horace Albright, the Acting Director of the National Park Service, made his first trip to Zion. When Albright arrived in Cedar City he was surprised to find a crowd waiting for him to make a speech. "I gave them a rousing, impromptu speech... about the beauties of Utah (which I hadn't yet seen)...We spent the next uncounted hours bouncing and crashing over some of the worst roads I had ever experienced...Convict labor had been used to make these so-called roads. Those men probably took out their hate and frustration on these projects." Seeing Zion, Albright was "surprised, excited, and thrilled...From day one it was a personal crusade to mold it from a little national monument into a great national park." But it would take something special before the road to Zion was improved. What happened?

1) A flash flood wiped out the old road.
2) A president of the United States visited Zion.
3) Henry Ford donated the money for a new road.

A. 2) A Zion visit by President Warren Harding in 1923 prompted the state of Utah to send 200 workers (non-convicts) to improve the road to Zion. Harding rode the first train on the new spur line to Cedar City. When Horace Albright communicated his enthusiasm about Zion to his boss, Stephen Mather, the Director of the National Park Service, Mather wondered if Albright had been drunk. Mather had never seen Zion. But when Mather saw Zion for himself a couple of years later, he too became enchanted by it, and he donated $5,000 of his own money to help build another road to Zion.

The first tourist lodgings in Zion Canyon were set up in 1917 by William Wylie. In 1893 Wylie had set up the first tourist camp in Yellowstone. His camp consisted of tent cabins, which had wooden frames, floors, and roofs, but canvas walls. Wyile also served meals. When the Union Pacific Railroad wanted to set up the first tourist facilities in Zion, Bryce Canyon, and the North Rim of the Grand Canyon, it turned to Wylie. William Wylie himself ran his camp in Zion.

An important backer of both Zion and Bryce Canyon was Utah's Senator Reed Smoot, who in 1916 introduced the bill creating the National Park Service.

In 1916 Wylie sent his two sons and their wives on a car trip to scout out Bryce Canyon and the North Rim of the Grand Canyon for camps there. The roads were primitive and without any signs to guide the way. The Wylies got confused and followed the wrong road, ending up near Mt. Trumbull. The Wylies ran out of gas, then water. At night they spotted the campfire of a sheepherder and got help. This experience convinced the Wylie sons and their wives that this country was too remote and primitive for tourists or for themselves.

William Wylie did succeed at setting up a camp on the North Rim of the Grand Canyon, but he abandoned his plans for a camp at Bryce Canyon. The Wylie camps at Zion and the North Rim of the Grand Canyon lasted for a decade, and then the Union Pacific Railroad bought them out to build lodges on their locations.

Q. When Stephen Mather, the first director of the National Park Service, died in 1930, his admirers created a plaque in his honor and gave copies to many national parks and monuments. The plaque held an image of Mather and the inscription "There will never come an end to the good that he has done." Many parks installed their plaque in a special location. Zion's plaque was installed on a large boulder in an alcove known as "The Stadium," about halfway up the Riverside Walk. This plaque was three feet long and made of bronze, making it quite heavy. Yet one day around 1950, this plaque disappeared. What had happened to it?
1) It was swept away by a flash flood.   2) It was stolen.
3) A rockslide buried it.

A. 1) It was swept away by a flood—but not a flood of the Virgin River, which isn't very close to the Stadium. The plaque was right below a cliff that flows with waterfalls during heavy rains. A waterfall knocked the plaque off its boulder and buried it under so much sand that it took a metal detector to find it. Today this plaque is located in front of the Human History Museum. Bryce Canyon's Mather plaque is located in front of its visitor center.

In 2002, the Olympic torch was carried through Zion National Park on its way to the Salt Lake City Winter Olympics.

In 1930 **Polly Mead Patraw** became only the second female ranger-naturalist in the history of the National Park Service.  Her career was inspired, in part, by Zion and Bryce Canyon. Polly was studying botany at the University of Chicago in 1927 when she made a summer-long field trip to Yellowstone, Zion, Bryce Canyon, and the Grand Canyon.

"I was so thrilled about Zion," she recalled. "I had never seen country like that. I thought 'wouldn't it be wonderful to live in a place like that?'" Polly spent the next two summers on the North Rim of the Grand Canyon, doing botany research for her master's thesis. In 1930 she became a ranger at the Grand Canyon. Soon she won the heart of the park's assistant superintendent, Preston Patraw, and they got married. In 1932 Preston Patraw was appointed the third superintendent of Zion National Park. It was Preston who gave Checkerboard Mesa its name.

Polly continued her botanical research at Zion, identifying 30 new plant species there, and some at Bryce Canyon. She loved living at Zion: "The houses at Zion were built of red sandstone. You know how we like to have everything fit in with the scenery? I was a good Park Service wife: both of our children, George and Betsy, had red hair and fit in with the scenery."

Q. When Zion became a national park in 1919, the National Park Service wanted to make it more accessible from the east, the direction of Bryce Canyon and the Grand Canyon. To get through Zion's massive eastside cliffs, engineers created the Zion-Mt. Carmel Highway and Tunnel. The tunnel is 1.06 miles (1.7 km) long. When it was finished in 1930 it was one of the longest highway tunnels in the United States. Today, nearly a century later, where does Zion's tunnel rank among land highway tunnels in the United States (as opposed to railroad or underwater tunnels)?
1) #3   2) #8   3) #15
A. 2) It's now #8.

In 1958 a pillar inside the Zion-Mt. Carmel Tunnel collapsed, dropping tons of debris into the tunnel. The tunnel then was reinforced with concrete ribs.

Q. While national parks are all about the wonders of nature, a few engineering feats in national parks have become wonders in their own right. Two of the most famous are the Going-to-the-Sun Highway in Glacier National Park, and the Zion–Mt. Carmel Highway and Tunnel. Both roads were built in the 1920s to make the parks accessible to automobiles. The Going-to-the-Sun Highway is 53 miles (85 km) long and climbs 3,000 feet (914 m) over the Continental Divide. The Zion–Mt. Carmel Highway is 24 miles (38 km) long.

On a per-mile basis, which highway was more expensive to build?
A. The Zion–Mt. Carmel Highway cost $78,000 per mile, while the Going-to-the-Sun Highway cost $47,000 per mile. The Zion–Mt. Carmel Highway was more expensive because of the tunnel. The tunnel cost $503,000 in 1928, which is about $6 million in today's dollars. The cost of the entire highway was $1.9 million, or about $25 million in today's dollars. Nearly half of this total was for the switchbacks below the tunnel. They climb 800 feet (243 m) in 3.6 miles (5.8 km). They required the moving of nearly five times the amount of debris removed from the tunnel.

Q. How many tons of dynamite were used to create the tunnel?
1) 12   2) 76   3) 146
A. 3) 146 tons, or 292,320 pounds (132,594 kg). This comes to 4.06 pounds (1.8 kg) of explosives per cubic yard of rock removed. In all, 72,000 cubic yards of rock was removed. On an average day, the blasting and drilling advanced 20.6 feet (6.3 m).

Q. When dynamite went off, workers who were eating in the dining hall below would drop their food and rush over to the walls and stand there a few moments, then return to the tables to eat. Why did they do this?
A. One time, a blast on the cliffs above shot out a 10-pound (4.5 kg) sandstone rock, which crashed through the dining-hall roof and landed on the dining-room table while workers were seated around it.

The U.S.S. Bryce Canyon *was a navy ship, a destroyer-tender, that sailed the Pacific Ocean from 1946 to 1981.*

Q. The tunnel runs inside the cliff, no more than 40 feet (12 m) inside it. At six points along the way, workers added a "gallery," an opening from the tunnel, with a view of Zion's cliffs outside. Why were these galleries added?
1) For the view   2) Ventilation for the workers
3) To create exits for bats

A. 2) Ventilation for the workers. Working inside a mile-long tunnel full of dynamite fumes and dust would have been very unhealthful without a source of fresh air. Originally there were six galleries, but one of them allowed water to drip into the tunnel, which in winter became ice, so this gallery was plugged with concrete. When the highway and tunnel were dedicated on July 4, 1930, the largest gallery was used for the dedication ceremony, which drew 2,000 people, including the governors of twenty U.S. states. In the early years when there wasn't much traffic, drivers could park in a gallery and admire the view, and rangers gave talks there. Many of the construction workers soon went to help build Hoover Dam.

Twice, Zion National Park has been a pioneer at how to arrange transportation in national parks. In the 1920s the National Park Service was eager to open up the national parks to the new era of the automobile, which was why it

built the Zion-Mt. Carmel Highway and Tunnel. This highway proclaimed that nothing could stop cars from reaching national parks.

Nothing, that is, except the cars themselves. By the 1980s, Zion had become the national model of a national park with too many cars. Zion Canyon is a narrow place, and there isn't room to build parking for everyone. On an average summer day in the 1990s, thousands of cars were competing for about 450 parking spaces.

This wasn't the kind of experience for which people come

During World War II, the lodges at Zion and Bryce Canyon closed for over three years. To deter sabotage of the Zion-Mt. Carmel Tunnel, security was increased, including a night watchman.

to national parks. There were fist fights over parking spaces.
The answer was Zion's shuttle bus system, started in 2000. Now visitors can relax and enjoy the view, and they see a lot more wildlife, which used to be scared off—and killed off—by all the cars. A rider on a shuttle bus uses one-third the energy of a person in a car.

Q. For the 100th anniversary of Zion becoming a national monument, in 2009 a commemorative coin was made. One of these coins had an unusual adventure. What was it?
1) It went into space on a space shuttle.
2) It was used for the coin toss at the Super Bowl.
3) It hit a big jackpot in Las Vegas.
A. 1) In February of 2010, the Zion coin went into space on the space shuttle *Endeavor*. It was taken by astronaut Robert Behnken, an admirer of Zion National Park.

Q. Who were the first European-Americans to see Bryce Canyon?
A. In 1866 Captain James Andrus led a group of Mormon militia just beneath Bryce Canyon. In 1872 geologist Grove Karl Gilbert "caught a glimpse of a perfect wilderness of red pinnacles, the stunningest thing out of a picture." In 1873 Almon Thompson became the first known Euro-American to explore Bryce Canyon from the top of its plateau. Thompson was a U.S. government surveyor; years later he helped start the National Geographic Society.

Bryce cabin, now in Tropic, Utah

Q. Bryce Canyon was named for Ebenezer and Mary Bryce, who homesteaded below Bryce Canyon in 1875. But Mary Bryce's health required a warmer climate, so after five years they moved to Arizona. What did Ebenezer think of Bryce Canyon? We know only one line he reportedly said about it. What was it?
1) "It's a hell of a place to lose a cow."
2) "It's the most beautiful place on Earth."
3) "Someday this place will become a national park."
A. 1) "It's a hell of a place to lose a cow."

The Bryce Canyon Scenic Drive originally ended at Sunset Point; in the 1930s the CCC extended it to Rainbow Point.

Q. Because of its remote location, Bryce Canyon remained unknown to the public even longer than did Zion. In 1915, J.W. Humphrey became the U.S. Forest Service supervisor in the Bryce Canyon area. Having come from Moab, Humphrey thought he'd seen the best scenery Utah had to offer, but he was astonished to discover Bryce Canyon: "It was sundown before I could be dragged from the canyon view." Humphrey led a campaign to make Bryce Canyon a national monument. He often took visitors to Bryce Canyon by horseback, charging them $1, but he guaranteed that if they were disappointed with Bryce Canyon, he would refund their money. He never needed to refund anyone's money. In June, 1923, President Warren Harding signed the bill making Bryce Canyon a national monument. How many people visited Bryce Canyon in its first year as a national monument?

1) 3,692   2) 17,213   3) 55,997

A. 2) 17,213. This was a lot more than had visited Zion in its first year as a national park (only 3,692). By 1923, the Union Pacific Railroad had started bus tours of Zion and Bryce Canyon. Signing the Bryce Canyon bill was almost the last thing Warren Harding did in the White House. Soon after, he left on a long tour of the western U.S., including Zion, but not Bryce Canyon. A few weeks after visiting Zion, Harding died of a heart attack.

The first lodge at Bryce Canyon was opened in 1920 by Reuben "Ruby" Syrett and his wife Minnie. Ruby was working in the area when a local rancher, Claude Sudweeks, told him he should go and see "a hole in the ground"—Bryce Canyon. (There's a historic photo of Sudweeks on his horse atop Bryce Canyon's Natural Bridge).

When Ruby and Minnie saw Bryce Canyon: "We stood speechless. The coloring, the rock formations, we'd never seen anything like it. What a surprise the hole turned out to

Almon Thompson, the first Euro-American explorer of Bryce Canyon, was the brother-in-law of John Wesley Powell, the first explorer of the Colorado River by boat.

be! We thought everyone should see it, so from this time on we took our friends there."

Ruby and Minnie got into the tourist business by accident. For some visiting friends, Ruby and Minnie set up a tent on the canyon rim, and cooked meals. Their friends were delighted with the whole experience. Before Ruby and Minnie could take down the tent, some other tourists came along and asked for their services.

Ruby and Minnie decided to build a small lodge there that winter. They called it "Tourists' Rest." It was a log cabin, 30 feet by 71 feet (9 x 22 m), including a dining room and  fireplace. It was located near today's Bryce Canyon Lodge. Outside, Ruby cut a tree stump into a giant bath tub.

In 1923 the Union Pacific Railroad bought out Ruby's business to build Bryce Canyon Lodge. Ruby and Minnie set up a new lodge on their ranch outside the park boundary, where it has grown to become today's giant Ruby's Inn.

Q. In its tourist booklet, the Union Pacific Railroad suggested that visitors to Bryce Canyon should get their first view of  Bryce Canyon in the same way that Stephen Mather, the first director of the National Park Service, first saw Bryce Canyon. What was this?

1) Close your eyes and have someone lead you to the rim, then open your eyes for a big surprise.

2) Have a picnic on the rim.

3) See it at sunset.

A. 1) When Stephen Mather first visited Bryce Canyon in 1919, a friend of his drove him toward the rim and told Mather to close his eyes and keep them closed until they got there. When Mather opened his eyes, he gasped in wonder. He also promised to make Bryce Canyon a national park.

Stephen Mather in Zion, 1920

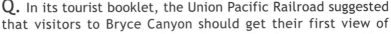

The year 1928, when Bryce Canyon became a national park, was also when Walt Disney created Mickey Mouse, Amelia Earhart became the first woman to fly the Atlantic, and Ty Cobb got his final baseball hit.

Q. Just as Zion has an amazing engineering feat (the Zion-Mt. Carmel Highway and Tunnel), Bryce Canyon too has its own large engineering project, though it's not so obvious. In the 1880s pioneers living east of Bryce Canyon realized they couldn't rely on the Paria River for water, so they spent two years building a ditch system to bring water from the west side of Bryce Canyon, where they built a reservoir. How long is this ditch system?
1) 5 miles   2) 10 miles   3) 25 miles

A. 3) 25 miles. Water flows from the Tropic Reservoir by gravity, flows past Ruby's Inn in pipes, and down Water Canyon. You can see this water flowing where it crosses Highway 12, at the Mossy Cave Trail.

Waterfall in Water Canyon, on the Mossy Cave Trail.

From their start, both Bryce Canyon and Zion have offered horseback rides.

Red Rock Culture
Movies, Architecture, Art, Music

Q. One of the most famous movie scenes involving any national park is the bicycle scene in *Butch Cassidy and the Sundance Kid*, a scene set to the song "Raindrops Keep Fallin' on My Head." This scene was filmed in the ghost town of Grafton, just outside Zion National Park, and it shows Zion landscapes in the background. The song, composed by Burt Bacharach, became a #1 hit and won the 1969 Academy Award for best song. True or false: the bicycle scene and song weren't in the original script; they were thrown in at the last minute.
A. True. The bicycle scene and song were added at the last minute to add some fun and romance between the characters played by stars Paul Newman and Katherine Ross.

Q. The old-fashioned bicycle used in *Butch Cassidy and the Sundance Kid* was supposed to be ridden by a stunt double for Paul Newman, since the trick-riding scene was considered too likely to injure the stars. But Newman soon proved that he could handle the trick riding. He rode Katherine Ross around on his handlebars, through bright flowers and flickering sunlight, a scene that helped the movie win its Academy Award for best cinematography. Of course, Zion's beauty should get some of the credit for that award. Two years later the movie company auctioned off the bicycle. Burt Bacharach wanted it, but he was outbid by a friend of Paul Newman. How much did the bicycle fetch?

1) $250   2) $1,200   3) $3,100

A. 3) $3,100. And that was in 1971 dollars. It would be more like $15,000 today.

Q. One famous movie star loved Zion so much that he used it as a background for three of his movies. Who was he?

1) Paul Newman   2) Robert Redford
3) Clint Eastwood

A. 2) Robert Redford. In addition to *Butch Cassidy and the Sundance Kid*, the other two movies were *Electric Horseman* and *Jeremiah Johnson*. Redford called Zion "A place drawn by God's own hand."

Robert Leroy Parker, alias Butch Cassidy, from a group portrait made with his gang in 1900.

While *Butch Cassidy and the Sundance Kid* was filmed near Zion, the real Butch Cassidy, who was born in southwest Utah in 1866, is known to have hidden out near Bryce Canyon, and also in the Canyonlands and Capitol Reef areas. At Capitol Reef a natural arch got named "Cassidy Arch." Just west of Bryce Canyon, as you drive through Red Canyon on Highway 12, you pass "Butch Cassidy Draw." (A draw is a big gully).

Q. Moviemaking in the town of Grafton started well before *Butch Cassidy and the Sundance Kid*, before Grafton was a ghost town—the last resident left around 1945. In 1928 part of *In Old Arizona* was filmed there. It was a western romance, with the promotional slogan "Two Men and a Senorita in a Rodeo of Love." What was special about this movie?

1) It was one of the first talking movies filmed outdoors.
2) It was based on a story by the famous writer O. Henry.

Maurice Cope, one of Bryce Canyon's first rangers, was a friend of Butch Cassidy.

3) It won the Academy Award for best actor for Warner Baxter, in only the second year the Academy Awards were presented.
4) All of the above.
A. 4) All of the above. The next year, Grafton hosted *The Arizona Kid*, once again starring Warren Baxter, plus Carole Lombard. In 1947 Veronica Lake starred in *Ramrod*, a cattlemen-versus-sheepherders saga, whose promotional slogan was "They Called it God's Country...Until the Devil Put a Woman There!"

Q. What Clint Eastwood movie was filmed inside Zion National Park?
1) *The Unforgiven*   2) *The Good, the Bad, and the Ugly*
3) *The Eiger Sanction*
A. 3) *The Eiger Sanction*. This was one of the first movies to feature the sport of climbing. To get ready to climb Switzerland's Eiger Mountain, Clint Eastwood trains in Zion Canyon. He jogs in the Narrows, on the Angels Landing Trail, and at Checkerboard Mesa. For climbing scenes, Eastwood didn't use a stuntman; he really did his own climbing. Some scenes show Eastwood hanging out at a swimming pool at Zion Lodge. This swimming pool was removed in 1975, but parts of its patio and rock wall are still visible today.

> *The Eiger Sanction* included a scene of Clint Eastwood climbing in Monument Valley, which is 150 miles (241 km) east of Zion, and viewers were left thinking this scene was in Zion. Hollywood movies often mix scenes from different places. The 1934 movie *The Dude Ranger*, made from the Zane Grey novel of that name, showed its heroes in Zion Canyon one moment, and on the rim of the Grand Canyon the next moment. It's as if the moviemakers thought that viewers wouldn't notice the difference. And in truth, as of 1934 only a small portion of the American public had visited Zion.

Q. In 1927 a Spanish hacienda was built at Zion's Temple of Sinawava. It was actually a set for a movie version of Helen Hunt Jackson's classic novel about prejudice against Native Americans. What was the name of this novel and movie?
1) *Uncle Tom's Cabin*   2) *Ramona*   3) *Dances with Wolves*

Bryce Canyon appears in the "rat pack" movie Sergeants 3, *along with a Hollywood set of fake hoodoos.*

A. 2) *Ramona*. The movie was a silent movie starring Dolores Del Rio. The next year she recorded the song "Ramona," which became a #1 hit for eight weeks and sold a million copies. *Ramona* was remade as a talking movie in 1936, starring Loretta Young, this time filmed near Kanab. The 1927 *Ramona* turned out to be a good deal for Zion National Park. When the movie set was disassembled, its Spanish roof tiles were stacked up, and they caught the attention of an electric company, which was looking for exactly such tiles for its new building in St. George. The National Park Service traded the tiles to the power company in exchange for their hooking

Dolores Del Rio in the 1920s.

up Zion to power from outside the park. Until 1927, Zion had its own electricity generation station in the Court of the Patriarchs.

Tom Mix in the Twenties.

Q. In the 1920s, cowboy star Tom Mix was filming a movie in Zion Canyon. The film crew had set up their camera in the best spot, but then they noticed that a tree branch was intruding into their shot. They told chief ranger Donal Jolley to cut down the tree branch, but Jolley refused. Then Tom Mix himself offered to give Jolley his cowboy hat if he would cut off the branch. What did Jolley do?

A. Jolley still refused. The movie crew had to move their camera. Jolley didn't get the cowboy hat. Some park rangers are so dedicated, they'll make great personal sacrifices for the sake of a tree.

In 2007 Bryce Canyon appeared in the movie *Bonneville*, starring Jessica Lange. After the death of her husband Joe, Lange and the daughter of Joe's first wife come into conflict over the disposition of Joe's cremation ashes. The daughter

Ramona was made into a movie four times, and since 1923 it's been an outdoor play near San Diego.

wants them buried beside Joe's first wife, but Lange had promised Joe to scatter his ashes in a wild, beautiful place. To deliver Joe's ashes to the daughter at Joe's funeral, Lange drives across the Southwest, recreating the route of her and Joe's honeymoon, a route they had talked about repeating someday. Lange stops at Bryce Canyon and stays at Bryce Canyon Lodge. At night she wanders out to the rim, carrying the container with Joe's ashes, and she sits enjoying the beauty of Bryce Canyon. We don't see what happens there, but at the end of the movie we discover that Lange has scattered Joe's ashes into Bryce Canyon.

Q. Both Zion Lodge and Bryce Canyon Lodge were designed by the same architect, Yale-educated Gilbert Stanley Underwood. Underwood also designed the lodges at the North Rim of the Grand Canyon and at Cedar Breaks National Monument. But none of these lodges is considered to be Underwood's greatest national-park lodge. Indeed, many fans of national-park architecture consider another of Underwood's lodges to be the best lodge in the entire national park system. Which lodge is this?

Zion Lodge

Bryce Canyon Lodge

1) Old Faithful Inn, in Yellowstone
2) The Ahwahnee Hotel, in Yosemite
3) El Tovar Hotel, on the South Rim of the Grand Canyon

A. 2) The Ahwahnee Hotel in Yosemite. People admire it for the way it honors nature, with its natural materials of stone and wood,

---

Gilbert Stanley Underwood designed a cafeteria at Zion, now the Nature Center near the South Campground.

its design motifs, and the way it blends into the landscape. With Zion Lodge, built in 1925, Underwood meant for its four tall sandstone pillars to symbolize the tall sandstone cliffs around it, and he used pine logs taken from the canyon rim. With Bryce Canyon Lodge, its stones were quarried from a mile away.

Q. Gilbert Stanley Underwood's first design for Zion Lodge was a giant building, three stories tall, with two long wings holding 75 guest rooms. But Stephen Mather, the director of the National Park Service, felt this design was so large it would compete against the natural scenery. Mather insisted on another arrangement, which is the arrangement you can see today at Zion, Bryce Canyon, and the North Rim of the Grand Canyon. What is this arrangement?

Underwood

A. A central building holds a lobby, a restaurant, a meeting hall for ranger talks, and a gift shop, while all the lodging is in cabins nearby. But many of Underwood's cabins at Zion were removed in the 1980s and replaced by motel-type units. Only 15 of the original cabins remain.

Q. Gilbert Stanley Underwood had great talent, but rotten luck. His Grand Canyon Lodge on the North Rim of the Grand Canyon, built at a cost of half a million dollars, lasted only five years before it was destroyed by fire. (It was rebuilt.) His Zion Lodge lasted 40 years, then it burned down in 1966. What was the cause of this fire?
1) Lightning   2) A tourist's cigarette   3) Construction workers
A. 3) Construction workers were using blowtorches to remove worn-out vinyl flooring. The only part of the lodge that survived was the fireplace in the auditorium. The lodge was rebuilt.

Q. Gilbert Stanley Underwood also designed a small lodge at Cedar Breaks National Monument. This lodge opened in 1924. It disappeared in 1972. What happened to it?
1) Fire 2) Earthquake   3) The National Park Service bulldozed it.
A. 3) The National Park Service bulldozed it. Because Cedar Breaks, at its 10,000-foot altitude, doesn't open until May and

---

Gilbert Stanley Underwood designed the Union Pacific Railroad's main station in Omaha, Nebraska.

doesn't have a long tourist season, the lodge was never profitable. In 1972 the lodge owners gave up on it and donated it to the National Park Service. In the 1970s, Americans hadn't yet developed a strong ethic of historic preservation. When Old Faithful Inn was showing its age in the 1970s, some people were willing to let it be torn down. Today, attitudes have changed a great deal. A good example of this is offered by Zion Lodge. When Zion Lodge burned down in 1966, it was quickly replaced—in only 108 days—but with plain, prefabricated walls. Many visitors who had loved the old Zion Lodge found the new lodge quite bland. In 1992, a historic renovation project restored the lodge exterior to Underwood's original rustic design.

Q. The roof of Bryce Canyon Lodge is much steeper than the roof of Zion Lodge. Why is this?

A. Bryce Canyon gets far more snow than Zion, so a steep roof helps the snow slide off. A steep roof is also consistent with Bryce Canyon Lodge's Swiss-Nordic style. The shingles on the lodge roof are stained green and cut and aligned in a wavy pattern, a unique design found in no other national park. Because Bryce Canyon is much cooler than Zion, Bryce Canyon Lodge needs no air conditioning.

The Five Eras of National Park Architecture

While national parks are mostly about nature, they are also rich in architecture, and they tell a story of how ideas about park architecture have changed over a century. In many of the larger national parks, you can see five eras of park architecture.

1. The railroad lodges. The first tourist facilities in many national parks were built by railroad companies, at a time when most Americans traveled by railroad. The railroads hired some brilliant young architects, who had inspired visions of how architecture could do justice to national parks, using natural materials and rustic design. The railroads spent a great deal of money building lodges with grandeur: Zion Lodge cost $334,000, or nearly $4 million in today's dollars.

2. Park Service Rustic. When national parks built their own buildings, they adopted a style known as "Park Service

---

The main part of Bryce Canyon Lodge was built in 1924, the wings in 1926, the auditorium in 1927, the deluxe cabins in 1927-1929.

Rustic," which used stone and wood, both outside and in their interior design. Stone was selected from local stone, so it would blend in. Wood was often left as round logs, as in pioneer log cabins, rather than as smoothed beams or walls. Good examples of this style at Zion and Bryce Canyon are the original visitor centers, which at Zion is located at the Grotto, and at Bryce Canyon, next to the General Store.

3. The CCC. The Civilian Conservation Corps was a 1930s Great Depression program that gave jobs to young men and supported their families back home. The CCC made a huge contribution to the national parks, building museums, roads, trails, campgrounds, pipelines, boundary fences, overlooks, outdoor exhibits, amphitheaters, and park offices. Most of their work has endured quite well: the CCC boys did sturdy stone masonry. About 200 CCC boys worked at Bryce Canyon in the summer and moved to Zion in the winter. At Cedar Breaks the CCC built the log visitor center still used today, but at Zion and Bryce Canyon their architectural work is less visible. At Zion they built the entrance-sign pillar at the south entrance, and the amphitheater at the South Campground. At Bryce Canyon they built the exhibit shelter at Rainbow Point.

4. Mission 66. In the 1950s park tourism soared, especially

Mission 66 style: Quarry Visitors Center at Dinosaur National Monument, Utah

by automobile. Park facilities built in the 1920s were being overwhelmed, so the National Park Service launched the Mission 66 program to build many larger facilities by 1966, the 50th anniversary of the National Park Service. Mission 66 coincided with the peak of the style of architecture called "modern," which emphasized steel and glass instead of stone and wood, and which discouraged ornamentation, and thus many Mis-

Ruby Syrett was hired to cut the logs used to build Bryce Canyon Lodge.

sion 66 buildings were bland and could have fit into a big-city downtown as easily as into a national park. At Zion, today's Human History Museum was built in 1960 as the Mission 66 visitor center. Bryce Canyon too had a Mission 66 visitor center, but in 2001 it was remodeled in a rustic style, with a wooden exterior and a steep green roof like the roof of Bryce Canyon Lodge.

5. The Environmental Era. By the 1970s the national parks were "being loved to death." They had big-city traffic headaches, and they had bulldozed miles of forests to build parking lots. This wasn't the purpose of national parks. The National Park Service developed a new philosophy of leaving new commercial developments outside park boundaries, of minimizing traffic stress, and of building green architecture. The new Visitor Center at Zion, built in 2000, is a leading example of this new philosophy. It returns to the rustic style, using stone and wood, yet it incorporates cutting-edge, energy-saving designs and technology. It is also the station for Zion's shuttle system.

Q. Most of the famous expeditions that explored the American West were accompanied by artists, not by photographers. Why was this?

A. Most of these expeditions had been finished by the 1870s, and at this time photography equipment was heavy, fragile, and difficult to use. Because cameras and glass photographic plates had to endure rough rides on horses or boats or backpacks, there were lots of ways to break them, and if you were in a remote wilderness, you were out of luck. By contrast, an artist required only a piece of paper and a pen or brush. Art could capture the color in the landscape, but black-and-white photographs could not. The first sketches of Zion and Bryce Canyon were done by John Weyss, an artist with the Wheeler survey in the 1870s.

Q. Art has played an important role not only in publicizing national parks, but in creating them. When artist Albert Bierstadt visited Yosemite in 1863, Yosemite was still fairly unknown to the American public. Bierstadt's paintings helped convince the Lincoln

---

Bryce Canyon Lodge, the only one of Gilbert Stanley Underwood's four Union Pacific Lodges still standing, was named a National Historic Landmark in 1987.

Administration that Yosemite deserved to be protected, which it was, at first, by the state of California. In the 1870s Thomas Moran accompanied government expeditions to Yellowstone and the Grand Canyon. Congress paid Moran $20,000 to do a giant painting of each place. These paintings were hung in the U.S. Capitol building and stirred up enthusiasm for the idea of national parks. Zion too owes its first national publicity to an important artist. He came to Zion in 1873 and made an engraving of it, which was

published in a national magazine. Who was this artist?
1) Albert Bierstadt   2) Thomas Moran
3) Thomas Hart Benton
A. 2) Thomas Moran. Moran said: "...for glory of scenery and stupendous scenic effects [Zion] cannot be surpassed...It is a marvelous piece of Nature's handiwork that is worth going a long distance to see."

Q. Art played an important role in the creation of Zion National

"Zion Valley" by Thomas Moran   Park. In 1871, at age seventeen, Frederick Dellenbaugh was part of the second expedition of John Wesley Powell down the Colorado River. Dellenbaugh first saw Zion soon after the Powell expedition. Thirty years later, now an accomplished artist, Dellenbaugh fell under the spell of Zion and said: "Not even the best part of the Grand Canyon offers a more varied spectacle." Dellenbaugh's paintings of Zion were displayed at the 1904 St. Louis World's Fair and captured the public imagination. They helped persuade President William Howard Taft to set aside Zion as a national monument five years later. In 1904 the population of the United States was about 80 million. How many millions of Americans attended the St. Louis World's Fair, and thus had a chance to see Dellenbaugh's paintings of Zion?
1) 4 million   2) 8 million   3) 20 million
A. 3) 20 million, or about one quarter of the American public. Stephen Mather, the first director of the National Park Service,

---

The rocking chairs in front of Zion Lodge are modeled after original 1920s hickory-pole chairs.

understood the power of art. The year after the National Park Service was created (in 1916), Mather organized a major showing of national-park art at the National Gallery of Art.

If you've ever seen the TV show *Antiques Road Show*, you know that valuable art can show up in the strangest places. This was the case for some of the most important art in the history of Zion National Park. In 2007 one of Frederick Dellenbaugh's paintings of Zion, which was exhibited at the 1904 St. Louis World's Fair, suddenly turned up in an antiques auction in Tennessee. Fortunately, officials at Zion National Park heard about it ahead of time, and the Zion National Park Foundation was able to raise the money to buy the painting for the park collection. Another important name in Zion and Bryce Canyon art history is Howard Russell Butler. In the early 1900s Butler was a well-known painter of landscapes and portraits. In 1926 the Union Pacific Railroad commissioned Butler to create  nine large paintings of Zion and Bryce Canyon. These paintings went on tour, and in New York City they won much praise. The paintings ended up in a museum in Buffalo, New York, where eventually they went into storage and were forgotten and damaged. In 1999 Zion National Park heard about these paintings and acquired them.

Q. The first artist to devote years to painting Zion was John Fairbanks. Born in Utah and trained in Paris, Fairbanks traveled to Zion in 1917 on an impulse, and ended up living in Springdale for years, painting Zion. What was it that made Fairbanks fall in love with Zion?
1) The red cliffs at sunset
2) The cottonwood trees in autumn
3) He fell in love with the daughter of a Springdale merchant.
A. 3) He fell in love with the daughter of a Springdale merchant.

The lodges in national parks are owned by the National Park Service, but operated by private companies.

Their son, Avard Fairbanks, also became an artist and painted Zion in the 1950s.

> Artists painting Zion in the 1920s and 1930s found that the park's first ranger, Donal Jolley, was very sympathetic to their efforts. Sometimes he provided them with the supplies they needed, and in exchange they gave him paintings. Over the years, Jolley's house filled up with paintings. This must have made an impression on his son, for his son later became a professional artist and enjoyed painting Zion.

Q. One of the most famous artists associated with Utah is Maynard Dixon. In 1933, Dixon and his wife (and famous photographer) Dorothea Lange left their San Francisco home to seek peace and inspiration in the Utah Desert. Dixon and Lange spent two months in and near Zion, and Dixon painted nearly 40 paintings. Dixon was so enthralled by Zion, what did he do?

1) He built a house a dozen miles outside the park, so he could paint Zion often.
2) He became a national park ranger at Zion.
3) He painted murals inside Zion Lodge.
A. 1) In 1939 he built a house in the village of Mt. Carmel, just north of Mt. Carmel Junction. For the last six years of his life Dixon spent long summers at Mt. Carmel. In all, he painted 200 paintings of Utah landscapes, including Zion and Bryce Canyon. Today Dixon's home at Mt. Carmel is open for tours.

Q. When Maynard Dixon was driving into Zion in 1939 with his family, they were half-way through the mile-long Zion-Mt. Carmel Tunnel when their car headlights stopped working. In the dark, they couldn't see where they were going, and oncoming traffic couldn't see them. What did they do?
A. They got newspapers out of the trunk, twisted them into torches, and lit them on fire. With his two sons riding on either side of the hood and holding the torches, they drove out of the tunnel.

Maynard Dixon's wife, Dorothea Lange, became famous for her photographs of Great Depression victims.

Q. One night when Maynard Dixon was in Zion, he and his son climbed high up on a ledge so that Dixon could sketch the canyon by moonlight. They camped on the ledge overnight, with a campfire for warmth. When they awoke, they found that several rattlesnakes had been attracted to their campfire embers and were still curled up next to them. What did Dixon do?

A. Dixon and his son waited for the morning sun to warm up the snakes, and then the snakes crawled away.

In the 50 years after Thomas Moran drew Zion in the long-established style of Romantic landscape painters, the art world saw a flurry of major innovations in style, such as impressionism, surrealism, and cubism. Considering how far away Zion and Bryce Canyon were from Paris, the capital of the art world, it's amazing how fast some of these new styles found their way to Zion and Bryce Canyon. This was mainly due to European artists who moved to America.

A good example of this is Swedish-born, Paris-trained Birger Sandzen. Sandzen developed a colorful, energetic painting style that reminds most people of Van Gogh. Critics dismissed Sandzen's colors as impossibly bright. But when Sandzen discovered Utah landscapes, he felt they justified his style: "There can be no danger of exaggerating nature's colors." In the 1920s Sandzen taught summer classes at two Utah colleges, where he influenced a generation of Utah-born artists, who were soon applying the latest Paris art styles to Utah landscapes. European artists like Sandzen felt like prospectors who had struck gold: "What a world of beauty waiting for interpretation in story, verse, color, and line."

Q. Max Ernst was a German painter who became famous in the 1930s for his surrealistic paintings, full of dream-like images. When Ernst finally came to America and saw southwestern landscapes, he said that they were just like the imaginary landscapes he had been painting for years—or even stranger. Ernst was so enthralled by the Southwest that he settled in Sedona, Arizona. In 1946 *Time* magazine held a contest called "Camera vs. Brush" to decide whether a photographer or an artist was better at making "unbelievable realities believable." The photographer was Ansel

---

Gilbert Stanley Underwood designed the now-gone swimming pool at Zion Lodge, filmed in Clint Eastwood's The Eiger Sanction.

Adams, famous for his photos of Yosemite. The artist was Max Ernst, whose entry was a painting of Bryce Canyon, in his usual eerie style. Who was declared the winner?

A. Ansel Adams. Commissioned by the National Park Service, Adams photographed Zion and Bryce Canyon in the 1940s.

Q. Who was the first person to photograph Zion Canyon?

A. Charles Savage, a Salt Lake City photographer who accompanied Mormon leader Brigham Young to Zion in 1870. But it was Jack Hillers whose photos helped make Zion famous. Hillers came

Jack Hillers

to Zion in 1872, after being the official photographer on the second expedition of John Wesley Powell down the Colorado River. Hillers went on to a long career with the U.S. Geological Survey, photographing much of the Southwest. The year after Hillers visited Zion, William Louis Crawford was born in Rockville, just outside of Zion Canyon. Crawford made his living farming and herding sheep, but his hobby was photography. He took his camera everywhere, even while herding sheep, and he built a home darkroom. His hundreds of photos are an invaluable record of Zion history, including the early years of national-park tourism.

Even today, the colors of Bryce Canyon can seem unreal to people. When the Bryce Canyon Natural History Association sent a book about Bryce Canyon to Hong Kong to be printed, the printers assumed that the colors in the photographs had to be wrong, so they readjusted them. The Bryce Canyon Natural History Association had to reassure the printers that Bryce Canyon really did look that strange and intense, and the books were redone.

Q. What is the artist-in-residence program?

A. Nearly a century ago American colleges originated the idea of the artist-in-residence, which brought prominent artists, writers, and musicians to campus and allowed students and faculty to ben-

The original Zion Lodge included an organ, played at dinnertime.

efit from their talents. In exchange, the artists got time to spend on creative activity. In 1984, Rocky Mountain National Park became the first national park to try out an artist-in-residence program. By 2010, 44 national parks had them. Competition for residencies is high, so those selected are often accomplished artists. Artists are required to give public presentations for park visitors or donate some of their work to the park. At Zion, the old visitor center at the Grotto is the residence for the artist-in-residence.

In the early 1930s the Colorado Plateau had its own Thoreau, a young man who left civilization to spend his time immersed in nature. Everett Ruess was still in his teens when he started four years of wandering. Everett was an artist and poet. In 1931 he visited Zion, but only after having a terrible time coaxing his burro to walk through the long, dark Zion-Mt. Carmel Tunnel. In 1934 Everett saw Bryce Canyon, which he called "grotesque and colorful formations." In the town of Tropic he stayed with park ranger Maurice Cope, and he rode a horse to help the Copes search for a missing cow. Then Everett moved on to the Escalante Canyons, where a week later he wrote the last letter anyone ever received from him. Everett vanished forever, at age 20. Yet Everett's writings and art, his sense of rapport with the landscape, and his joy at being alive, have continued winning the admiration of people who love the Colorado Plateau. His mysterious disappearance added to his mystique. In 2009 there was a flurry of media reports that Everett's bones had been found, but on more thorough investigation, this turned out to be a mistake.

Q. Bryce Canyon National Park has Shakespear Point, and Kodachrome Basin State Park, just east of Bryce Canyon, has Shakespeare Arch. Were these named for playwright William Shakespeare?
A. No, they were named for a local family. Some of them spell their name with an "e" on the end, and some without the "e." The local Shakespeares have traced their ancestry to Stratford-on-Avon in England, the hometown of William Shakespeare. But William Shakespeare had no children, so the Bryce Canyon Shakespeares can't be descended directly from him. In the late 1800s a William Shakespear started a ranch just below Shakespear Point; some

---

In the Great Depression, a public-works program hired artists to create posters of national parks to encourage tourism.

of his descendants have worked for Bryce Canyon National Park, and one, Harmon Shakespear, selected the trees used in building Bryce Canyon Lodge. It is appropriate that southwest Utah has landmarks named Shakespeare, since Cedar City hosts one of America's most respected Shakespeare theater festivals.

Q. Have any famous writers visited Zion and Bryce Canyon?
A. Surprisingly, John Muir, who would have loved the "sandstone Yosemite" of Zion Canyon, never visited Zion or Bryce Canyon. Utah-born poet May Swenson imagined Zion as "chiseled by giant tomahawks." Poet William Stafford, in his poem "Kolob Canyon," called Zion's cliffs "bulwarks too lofty to believe." In 1938 novelist Thomas Wolfe, author of *You Can't Go Home Again*, drove out of California's Mojave Desert and was delighted by the contrast of Zion's river and greenness. Bryce Canyon reminded him of stick candy, a "child's fantasy of heaven." Wolfe loved the "singaway," in which Union Pacific lodge employees sang a song of farewell to a bus of departing tourists. Wolfe noticed that four tourists in one group were so touched by the singaway that they had tears in their eyes. Wolfe hoped to write a book about Zion and Bryce Canyon and the rest of the West, but only weeks later he caught pneumonia and died.

Zion Lodge singaway in the 1950s

Q. What was the "singaway"?
A. The singaway started in the 1920s, soon after the opening of the Union Pacific lodges at Zion, Bryce Canyon, Cedar Breaks, and the North Rim of the Grand Canyon. No one is sure how the singaway started, but it fits right in with lodges that were so isolated that the employees had to provide their own entertainment, both for themselves and the guests. The lodge job application included a line for "Talents," and this was sometimes the most important skill. Each park put on its own show for guests, including musical instruments, songs,

The singaway was so popular, it was made into a record.

dances, jokes, and skits. At Zion, performers pretended their show was a live radio broadcast called "Sunset Serenade." Bryce Canyon did the "State Show," which included all 48 states in song and story and ended with Uncle Sam arriving for a patriotic sing-along. For the singaway, employees lined up outside the lodge, some with guitars and accordions. Each park had its own songs. At Bryce Canyon Lodge the lines included: "Merrily we roll away, we're sorry to see you go...We're glad you came to see our glorious canyon. Take one last look, the memory will remain till you come back to Bryce again." But bus tours declined to a small part of park visitation, and in the 1970s the singaway finally died out.

Q. Have Zion and Bryce Canyon inspired any famous music?
A. Olivier Messiaen of France was one of the great innovators of classical music in the 20th century. Messiaen loved nature, and  he considered Zion, Bryce Canyon, and Cedar Breaks to be "the greatest and most beautiful marvels of the world." He was inspired to write a symphony about them. To prepare, Messiaen spent eight days at Bryce Canyon, hiking its trails and transcribing its bird calls. Messiaen loved birds and astronomy, so he wove them into his work. The result was *Des Canyons Aux Ètioles*, or *From the Canyons to the Stars*. It premiered at Lincoln Center in New York City in 1974. The audience loved it, but Messiaen complained: "The New York critics clearly didn't understand...my admiration for the red-orange color of the rocks in Bryce Canyon. I wonder if they understand that the beauty of America is not concentrated only in the New York skyscrapers." But the people of Utah appreciated Messiaen's tribute, and they renamed a mountain near Cedar Breaks as Mount Messiaen. The title of Messiaen's work was prophetic, for Bryce Canyon National Park was soon to become the national leader in presenting astronomy to the public. And this brings us to the subject of our next chapter...

Olivier Messiaen's Canyons *symphony includes the song of the canyon wren, which many people consider the most magical bird call of canyon country.*

Cosmos National Park
Bryce Canyon and the Story of Astronomy in the National Parks

Q. As the National Park Service has matured, its sense of purpose has expanded. The first national parks were established mainly for the sake of geology—for spectacular mountains, canyons, valleys, volcanoes, glaciers, and geysers. Later, national parks were established for the sake of biology—for wildlife, forests, and wetlands. Recently, the National Park Service has decided that its mission should include astronomy—showing park visitors the night sky. The national park that has pioneered astronomy programs is Bryce Canyon National Park. Why is Bryce Canyon a perfect national park for astronomy?
A. Bryce Canyon has some of the darkest night skies in the United States.

Q. Why does Bryce Canyon have such good skies for viewing the stars?
1) High altitude   2) Low humidity   3) Remoteness from city lights and air pollution   4) Absence of clouds   5) All of the above
A. 5) All of the above. Bryce Canyon has a perfect combination of assets for astronomy. Bryce Canyon's 8,000-foot (2,440 m) el-

evation means that starlight is filtered by a mile-and-a-half (2.4 km) less atmosphere than it would be at sea level. Dry air means that star images are clear and steady, not blurred by humidity. Remoteness from cities means that there is little human-made light to compete with starlight, and little air pollution. The desert Southwest has fewer clouds than other regions: the Bryce Canyon night sky is clear for 152 nights per year, or over 40 percent of the time—more often in summer than winter. Famous astronomical observatories are built atop mountains that have viewing conditions similar to Bryce Canyon's.

Q. In the night skies of most of the rural United States, a person can see about 2,500 stars. But the skies at Bryce Canyon are so clear that you can see a lot more stars. How many?
1) 3,500   2) 5,000   3) 7,500
A. 3) 7,500 stars, at least on a moonless night.

Q. What does Bryce Canyon National Park do to present astronomy to the public?
A. Three times a week in the summer, rangers offer evening programs about astronomy, ranging from Native American sky legends to

the latest findings of the Hubble Space Telescope. Rangers also set up high-quality telescopes behind the Visitor Center so the public can view the sky. Once a year, Bryce Canyon hosts a four-day Astronomy Festival. Every month during the full moon, rangers lead "Full-moon hikes" on the canyon rim and down a trail

Sun-viewing at Bryce, with a safe telescope

among the hoodoos. Every month in summer, a NASA representative gives programs about space exploration. The Visitor Center includes a "star chamber," a dark rotunda in which you can see a glowing Milky Way and many constellations. Outside the Visitor Center is a "planet walk," with signs that give you a sense of the scale of the

---

Bryce Canyon started its astronomy programs in 1969, the same year humans first walked on the moon.

solar system. These days many other national parks are offering astronomy programs, but Bryce Canyon is still the best at it.

Q. The Bryce Canyon park rangers who present astronomy programs have a nickname. What is it?
1) Dark Rangers   2) Astro-Nuts   3) Bryce Owls
A. 1) Dark Rangers.

Q. Bryce Canyon's annual Astronomy Festival, held every July, is also called a "star party." What goes on at a star party?
A. A star party is a public event at which amateur astronomers set up telescopes for viewing the night sky. Bryce Canyon's Astronomy Festival offers as many as 40 telescopes. These are "backyard" telescopes, which are very high-tech, powerful instruments that reveal the night sky far beyond the capability of the human eye. During the day, you can see other "stars," guest speakers like astronaut Story Musgrave. Grand Canyon National Park has a star party every June, on both the south and north rims. Zion National Park doesn't have a star party, since its tall cliffs and tall trees make it harder to see the sky.

Q. What's the most popular object for viewing at star parties?
1) Mars   2) Saturn   3) The moon
A. 2) The big favorite is Saturn, with its rings. While humans easily see Saturn with the naked eye, humans never suspected that Saturn had rings until the telescope was invented. Star parties are usually held when there is no moon in the sky, since the moon is so bright that it washes out many fainter objects. Other popular objects for viewing are galaxies, nebulae, other planets and their moons, double stars, and—occasionally—comets.

Q. What happens on a "Full-moon hike"?
A. Even if you don't care about astronomy, you may still love a full moon hike at Bryce Canyon, for you will see the hoodoos in their most magical light. Full-moon hikes even go down a trail below the rim. Along the hike, rangers may share moon lore, point out constellations, or play recordings of the sounds of night creatures like owls. Full-moon hikes have become popular events at many national parks. At Grand Canyon National Park the ranger may tell

One Bryce Canyon telescope is named Thor, for the famous hoodoo. The telescope is large and red.

you how the Apollo astronauts, training for their flights to the moon, hiked to the bottom of the Grand Canyon to study geology. Apollo 16 astronaut Charlie Duke said: "The moon was out and the walls of the canyon were silhouetted in its light. Lying in my sleeping bag, I was transfixed by this magnificent sight above me. I couldn't help wondering if one day I might actually set foot on that moon."

In 1924 Congressman Louis Cramton of Michigan stayed at Bryce Canyon Lodge, and a clerk urged him to see the canyon by moonlight. The hoodoos at night reminded Cramton of a mysterious city. Cramton was so inspired that when he got back to Washington, D.C. he gave a speech about it:

"The ordinary schedule of my waking and sleeping was shattered, but that does not matter if you have but a day at Bryce...At midnight we cautiously approach the rim and watch, while far in the east over Acropolis Hill a glow enriches the

The Milky Way, viewed from Bryce Canyon

horizon. Soon a silver point of light comes to view, like a star of hope for a darkened city. Rapidly rises the majestic moon that whitens the night and brings out formless shapes of the city...It is a spectral city, and the watcher under the rays of the moon, the million wonders of the Milky Way, and all the stars overhead, comes to imagine an occasional moving in the tenantless homes. But there is nothing in the city but night." Cramton then urged that Bryce Canyon National Monument be promoted into a national park.

If you've never seen Zion by the light of a full moon, you're really missing something. It is, beyond doubt, one of the most beautiful visions in the world. Maynard [Dixon] painted it once, a beautiful painting, a deep and mysterious, almost reverent painting.

—John Dixon, son of painter Maynard Dixon

National parks now offer a Junior Ranger program devoted entirely to astronomy.

Night, the stars, the sun and moon, the elements, alone hold communion with that pristine crest [Zion]. Under its shadow we may almost touch the latch-string of Eternity; almost see ourselves in the dull mirror of Time.
—Frederick S. Dellenbaugh

Q. Almost all of the paintings done of Zion and Bryce Canyon are in the daylight. After all, artists are attracted to Zion and Bryce Canyon because of their brilliant colors, and at night these colors are gone. But for one important artist, Howard Russell Butler, the night too held magic. In 1926 the Union Pacific Railroad commissioned Butler to spend the summer painting Zion and Bryce Canyon. The Union Pacific was expecting colorful paintings it could use to promote its new lodges and tours. Butler did seven paintings of Zion, but two of those were nighttime scenes of cliffs glowing with moonlight and starlight. Why was Butler so attracted to the night?
1) He was colorblind.   2) He loved owls and bats.
3) He worked for the U.S. Naval Observatory.
A. 3) Butler was famous for his paintings of astronomical scenes, some of them commissioned by the U.S. Naval Observatory. Butler also painted astronomical murals for the American Museum of Natural History in New York City. Butler understood the magic of the night. He often painted night scenes of other landscapes.

Even with the naked eye, if the sky is dark enough, you can see the Andromeda galaxy, which in its size and spiral shape is nearly a twin of our own Milky Way galaxy. A galaxy is a system of many billions of stars. The Andromeda galaxy is our next-door neighbor galaxy, yet it is still so far away that its light takes over two million years to arrive on Earth. If you attend a star party you can look through telescopes and see galaxies that are ten million or twenty million light-years away. You can see light that was born before there was a Zion Canyon, a Bryce Canyon, or a Grand Canyon. During all the time this light has been flying through space, these canyons were being born and growing deeper and larger.

Q. The Milky Way is one of the most magnificent sights in the sky: a band of light that stretches across the whole sky. It's even more

*Mars has a canyon 3,000 miles (4,827 km) long,
over 300 times the length of Zion Canyon.*

interesting when you realize that you are seeing our own galaxy. But due to light pollution, a large percent of Americans can no longer see the Milky Way. What percent cannot see it?
1) 25 percent   2) 50 percent   3) 70 percent
A. 3) About 70 percent. For many city dwellers, national parks offer their first chance to see the Milky Way. Or meteors.

NASA satellite image of light pollution in North America and Europe

Q. "Light pollution" is the city lighting that prevents people from seeing the night sky. Professional astronomers have worried about light pollution for a long time. Mt. Wilson Observatory, which is where Edwin Hubble discovered the expanding universe, was rendered useless by the spreading lights of Los Angeles. While some lights are necessary for safety and crime prevention, many lighting fixtures are poorly designed, shooting half of their light into the sky, which serves no purpose. Light should be directed downward. How much money do Americans waste every year on light that is shot into the sky?
1) 100 million dollars   2) One billion dollars   3) Five billion dollars
A. 3) By some estimates, Americans could save five billion dollars every year by using better-designed lighting fixtures. They could also save their view of the night sky. The National Park Service now has a "Dark Sky Team" that studies lighting in national parks to encourage better lighting fixtures, and to educate nearby communities about their lighting. In 2008, the town of Bar Harbor, Maine, passed a light-pollution ordinance to protect next-door Acadia National Park. This Dark Sky Team started out at Bryce Canyon National Park. Excessive lighting can also interfere with the behavior of nocturnal animals, which need darkness for survival.

Q. The National Park Service also monitors air quality and air pollution in many national parks, especially where people expect

---

Venus is 900 F (482 C), the result of runaway global warming.

to see a great view of Earth scenery. In 1978, Bryce Canyon National Park installed cameras (such as the ones in the odd-looking shack behind Yovimpa Point) to take daily photographs of landmarks on the distant horizon; this allows measurement of how many miles people can see. Of national parks in the contiguous 48 states, where does Bryce Canyon rank for good air quality and long-distance views?
1) #2   2) #7   3) #10
A. 1) #2, behind Great Basin National Park. Bryce Canyon has a "median visibility" of 104 miles (167 km) in summer. The Grand Canyon scores 96 miles (154 km). Yosemite is 47 miles (75 km). The city of Los Angeles is only 12 miles (19 km). In fact, the largest source of air pollution at Bryce Canyon (and also at the Grand Canyon) is automobile pollution that has blown all the way from Los Angeles. Lack of air pollution is another reason why Bryce Canyon skies are great for astronomy.

Q. True or false: The rocks of Zion and Bryce Canyon are red for the same reason that the planet Mars is red.
A. True. Like Zion and Bryce Canyon, Mars has lots of iron. Under certain conditions, the iron in rocks can become concentrated into nodules. NASA's rovers *Spirit* and *Opportunity* found such iron nodules on Mars. Hikers find similar iron nodules in Zion National Park.

Q. In 2007 professional astronomers named an asteroid "Bryce Canyon." It is estimated to be three to five miles (5-8 km) across. Asteroids are chunks of stone and metal that are left over from the formation of the solar system. Where in the solar system do asteroids usually orbit?
1) Between Earth and our moon   2) Between Mars and Jupiter
3) Between Earth and Venus
A. 2) Between Mars and Jupiter.

Q. When NASA's *Cassini* spacecraft discovered geysers on Saturn's moon Enceladus, scientists named them for a landmark in one of the national parks. What name?
1) Thor's nostrils   2) The Great White Throne of Steam
3) Cold Faithful

On August 21, 2017, a total eclipse of the sun will pass directly through Grand Teton National Park and Great Smoky Mountain National Park.

A. 3) Cold Faithful, for Yellowstone's Old Faithful. The geysers on Enceladus shoot out just about the same amount of water as Old Faithful, about 8,000 gallons (30,320 liters), but because Enceladus has much less gravity than Earth, its geysers reach hundreds of miles high.

Artist's image of *Cassini* and Saturn

Q. What is "archaeoastronomy"?
A. This word combines the words "archaeology" and "astronomy." Archaeoastronomy studies both ruins and rock art to find astronomical features. Ancient peoples often knew the night sky better than modern people do. For them, the stars and planets were gods, whose comings and goings told humans when to plant crops or perform ceremonies. Ancient peoples sometimes incorporated astronomical sights and events into their buildings. They aligned windows to the sunrise on solstices—the longest and shortest days of the year. They placed rock art in the precise locations where a ray of light or a shadow would fall on the solstice. Archaeoastronomy can be a controversial subject, since some astronomical alignments will occur by chance. But there is plenty of convincing evidence that ancient peoples built major buildings like Stonehenge and Mayan pyramids with astronomical alignments. Zion National Park has a rock that casts a shadow in the shape of a coyote. On the summer solstice this shadow moves across a cliff face on which are engraved five petroglyphs, including two bird footprints. As it moves, the shadow mouth of the coyote eats the petroglyphs.

A mountain range on the moon is named "Smoky Mountains."

A Paiute Astronomy Legend

The Pleaides are a cluster of seven stars. To the Paiutes they are a family of seven Paiutes who took shelter in the sky during a terrible argument with Tu-rei-ris, the father of the family. When Tu-rei-ris saw them in the sky he threatened that if they didn't come down, he would turn them into *poot-sees* (stars) and they would never be able to come down. This is what he did. His family retaliated by turning him into a coyote. But Tu-rei-ris still loved and missed his family. This is why Coyote always looks up at the stars and howls sadly.

After William Wylie opened the first tourist facilities in Zion National Park, he opened a camp on the North Rim of the Grand Canyon in 1917, and he sent his daughter Elizabeth to manage it for the next ten years. But Elizabeth had wanted to be a professional astronomer. She attended Wellesley College, which has always had a strong astronomy program. Upon graduating in 1900, Elizabeth applied for a job at Lick Observatory in California, the leading observatory of the time. The director of Lick Observatory admitted that Elizabeth was just as qualified as the male applicants, but he turned her down—merely because she was a woman. At least, at the Grand Canyon Elizabeth enjoyed some of the darkest skies in America, skies better than the sky over Lick Observatory.

Chaco Canyon National Historical Park in New Mexico
has its own astronomical observatory building.

ADVENTURES
HIKING, CLIMBING, CANYONEERING

Q. What percent of visitors to Zion National Park go for a hike on a trail?
1) 20 percent   2) 50 percent   3) 70 percent
A. 3) 70 percent. This percentage was boosted by the creation of Zion's shuttle bus system, which it made it easier for people to reach trailheads. Half of that 70 percent hikes for at least two hours.

Q. Two of the most famous trails in the Southwest have the word "angel" in them. Which trail is steeper?
1) Angels Landing Trail in Zion
2) Bright Angel Trail in the Grand Canyon
A. 1) The Angels Landing Trail climbs 1,488 feet (453 m) in 2.4 miles (3.8 km), or 620 feet per mile (119 m per km). The Bright Angel Trail is "only" 561 feet per mile. Zion's Observation Point Trail is 537 feet per mile, and the Hidden Canyon Trail is 850 feet per mile.

Q. The Angels Landing Trail includes a steep set of 21 stone switchbacks called "Walter's Wiggles." Who was Walter?

A. Walter was Walter Ruesch, the son of Swiss immigrants, who was born in Springdale before Zion became a national monument. In 1916, Walter started working for the National Park Service as a laborer, and he became the monument custodian two years later. He took action to eliminate sheep grazing from monument lands. He hated wearing a uniform and wore one only when his superiors visited the park. In 1919, when Zion became a national park, Walter became acting superintendent. In 1925 he oversaw the building of the trail up to Angels Landing and the West Rim. The Wiggles have a 19 percent grade, with some spots up to 22 percent. In varying jobs, Walter worked at Zion until near his death in 1950.

> Joke: The Angels Landing Trail is highly recommended for the views. It's also recommended that while on the Angels Landing Trail, you *never look down!*

Q. Do Zion's cliffs ever collapse onto trails?
A. In 1968 a rockslide buried 250 feet (76 m) of the Riverside Walk under 20 feet (6 m) of debris, and several visitors were trapped upstream of the rockslide. One day a Zion ranger hiked up the Narrows, and on his way back he found that a bus-sized boulder had just fallen.

Q. The National Park Service closes the Zion Narrows to hiking when the Virgin River is flowing at 140 cubic feet per second,

or higher. But when you look at this level of water, it looks like it would barely come up to your knees. Is it really necessary to close the Narrows at this flow?
A. Yes: flowing water is a powerful force, which many people underestimate. Water up to your knees is enough to make walking very unstable, especially when you are walking over rounded, mossy rocks. To visualize a cubic foot of water, imagine a basketball full of water. A flow of 140 cubic feet per second (or "cfs") is equal to 140 basketballs flowing past you every second—with one or two of them hitting you. When

In 2010, Backpacker magazine ranked the Zion Narrows as one of the top ten hikes in the U.S.

you walk upstream from the mouth of the Narrows, the Narrows gets narrower, so the water gets deeper. In the springtime, water could reach up to your chest, and because this water is freshly melted snow, it's cold, creating a high risk of hypothermia. On the other hand, in the summer the cool water and the shade make the Narrows a delightful contrast with other hikes in the Southwest, which can be brutally hot. The Narrows is 20-30 F (11-17 C) cooler than the rest of Zion Canyon.

Q. The most popular national park for big-wall climbing is Yosemite. (A "big wall" is a very tall and sheer cliff.) Where does Zion National Park rank?
1) #2   2) #5   3) #12
A. 1) #2. Zion actually has more big-wall climbing routes than Yosemite. Climbing in Zion took off in the 1970s. In 1972 there were only 33 climbing attempts; in 1975, there were 118.

Q. For rock climbers, geology is no abstraction. Different types of rock have different characteristics, challenges, and dangers. In Zion Canyon, the lower cliffs are made of red rock, but the tops are made of white rock. Rock climbers dislike one of these colors, because it is weaker. As climbers try to grab the rock with their hands, they can feel the rock dissolving into dust or flaking off. Which layer is the weaker layer: the white or the red?
A. The white rock is the weaker rock, because it has less iron in it. Iron is what makes the red rock red, and iron also makes it stronger.

Great White Throne

Q. Who was the first person to climb the Great White Throne?
A. W.H.W. Evans, in 1927. Evans was a seasoned mountaineer, but also reckless. When told that it was impossible to climb the Great White Throne, he set out to climb it. He made it to the top, but on the climb back down he jumped over a small ledge, intending to catch a bush below, but "I must have missed it." He fell about 200 feet (61 m). Luckily, he landed on bushes and sand.

In 1985, Angels Landing Trail was paved with concrete to prevent erosion, and it took 285 helicopter flights to haul all the concrete.

He lay where he fell for 38 hours, unable to drink, since his canteen was so smashed he couldn't open it. Rangers organized a search for him, the first major search-and-rescue operation ever done in Zion National Park. They made a crude stretcher from logs, shoestrings, and the overalls of ranger Walter Reusch.

Q. When were other Zion peaks first climbed?
A. Angels Landing was first climbed in 1924 by David Dennett, a guide for Zion's horseback rides, and by park ranger Harold Russell. Cathedral Mountain was first climbed in 1931, West Temple in 1933, East Temple in 1937, and the Sentinel in 1938.

Q. If you are visiting Zion Canyon in the evening, you may see climbers who are still only halfway up a cliff. What's going to happen to them when it gets dark?
A. They "camp" right on a sheer cliff. They carry lightweight, fold-out platforms that they fasten onto the cliffs and sleep on.

Rock climbers are a colorful bunch of people, and so are the names they give to climbing routes. Here are some of the names of Zion climbing routes:

Cosmic Trauma	Better Safe than Sorry
Migraine	The Man Eater
Never Again	Tricks of the Trade
Enter the Dragon	Uncertain Fates
Barely Legal	Freak Show
Tree House of Horror	Sheer Lunacy
The Gypsy's Curse	

Q. In addition to climbing, Zion is famous for canyoneering. What's the difference between climbing and canyoneering?
A. In a word, climbing goes up while canyoneering goes down. Canyoneers descend into canyons, often very narrow slot canyons. Canyoneering involves rappelling down cliffs, swimming through huge, water-filled potholes, and scrambling up slopes and over boulders. Slot canyons are often hidden from the sun and very chilly, requiring wetsuits to swim through water, and they are prone to flash floods.

Hikers who hesitate to do the last half mile to Angels Landing can wait at the "widow's tree."

Q. Which is more dangerous: climbing or canyoneering?

A. With proper skills, equipment, experience, and common sense, neither activity needs to be dangerous. Climbers and

canyoneers aren't in it for the daredevil thrill of risking their lives, but for the athletic challenge and the immersion in nature. However, canyoneering leads to the most trouble. While the dangers of falling off a 2,000-foot (609 m) cliff are very obvious, many canyoneering beginners seriously

Canyoneers down at the bottom

underestimate the dangers of canyoneering. A large majority of the search-and-rescues in Zion National Park involve canyoneering.

Q. How high are the cliffs down which Zion canyoneers rappel?

A. The longest rappel in Zion is about 300 feet (91 m)—like a 30-story building. In most places, rappels cover a few dozen feet. Longer and more difficult slot canyons, with a series of drops, may take 30 or 40 rappels.

———

Canyoneering in Zion focuses on the sublime scenery and magnificent variety of natural forms, rather than on technical difficulty...The play of light upon the walls, the fluted and sculpted sandstone, the call of the canyon wren, the mystery of what is around the next corner—these are the wonders that the canyoneer delights in, that make Zion a magnificent playground.

—Tom Jones, longtime Zion canyoneer

Canyoneering Misadventures

1. Four young men used a hardware-store rope to descend into a canyon, only to discover that the rope was too short to reach the next level. They didn't know how to climb back up. The rangers who rescued them had to teach them how to climb up a rope.

2. In the month of April, when a slot canyon was cold and full of water, four canyoneers failed to wear wetsuits and were

Zion's Canyon Overlook Trail was built by the CCC, soon after the completion of the Zion-Mt. Carmel Highway and Tunnel.

soon freezing, but they didn't know how to climb back out.

3. A man was rappelling down a cliff when he found that his rope ended 15 feet (4.5 m) short of the canyon floor, and he fell this distance.

4. Many people have jumped into what they thought was a deep pool of water, only to find that it was only a foot deep. Many legs and ankles have been broken this way.

5. Some canyoneers, failing to read a map correctly, have gone down the wrong canyon, a far more difficult canyon than they could handle.

Q. Do climbers and canyoneers need to pass a test or possess a license to be allowed to go adventuring in national parks?

A. The pioneers who settled the American frontier didn't need a license, only a spirit of adventure—and skills. National parks are one of the few places left where this spirit of wilderness adventure is still welcome. But the National Park Service also expects people to bring skills and a sense of responsibility. Adventures like climbing, canyoneering, river running, and backpacking do require a permit, and these permits include a list of the hazards involved. The NPS employs backcountry rangers who offer expert advice on the difficulties of an adventure. However, it is not practical for the NPS to assess the skills of every adventurer and decide who is ready and who is not. Fortunately, serious climbers and canyoneers are a self-disciplined community. Every route is rated as to its difficulty, and people work systematically to improve their skills, so there is seldom a dangerous mismatch between a route and the skills required for it. Occasionally, nature and equipment play tricks on experienced adventurers. But the sad truth is that most accidents and fatalities happen to people who weren't prepared, or who took foolish chances.

Q. How many search-and-rescue operations do Zion National Park rangers conduct in an average year?

1) 46   2) 66   3) 86

A. 3) 86, or about one every four days. Rangers also perform 277 emergency medical services in an average year, for events like sprained ankles, heat exhaustion, or heart attacks.

Echo Canyon was a Native American trail, improved for livestock by pioneer John Winder.

Q. The desert Southwest might seem an unlikely place for flash floods, but in fact flash floods are often worse in canyon country than elsewhere. Why is this?

Flash flood aftermath in Zion Narrows

1) The topography funnels rain waters into narrow, steep canyons.
2) The rocky land can't absorb water.
3) There is little vegetation to absorb water.
4) Rain comes in intense thunderstorms.
5) All of the above.

A.   5) All of the above. Most flash floods in canyon country occur in the summer thunderstorm season (July, August, and September), which is when national parks have the most visitors.

Q. News reports about flash floods often refer to them as "a wall of water" that appears suddenly. True or false: flash floods really do have "a wall of water."

A. True. In canyon country, thunderstorms are so intense, and canyons funnel the water so tightly, that water really does pile up into a wall of water, sometimes many feet high. Even when floods happen without a wall of water, streams can rise very fast. In 2009, the Virgin River rose from 40 cfs to 500 cfs in only 45 minutes. The highest Virgin River flood ever recorded was 9,150 cfs. A big flash flood can move boulders and make the ground shake.

> How much does a flash flood weigh?
> One cubic foot of water = 62 pounds (28 kg)
> 1,000 cubic feet of water per second (cfs) = 62,470 pounds (28,111 kg) per second
> 1,000 cfs = 2.6 large elephants rushing past you every second

> Flash floods in canyon country can be so unpredictable that even park rangers have been caught by surprise. In her personal book, *Zion Canyon: A Storied Land*, longtime Zion ranger Greer Chesher tells of how she and five other Zion

Kayaking is allowed on the Virgin River, up to flows of 600 cfs, but not in the Narrows when hiking starts.

rangers were descending a long, steep, narrow Zion slot canyon when unseasonal thunderstorms sent a flood down the canyon, nearly sweeping them away. They survived by clinging to a narrow ledge all night long. Chesher described the nightmare scene: "The pouring rain rips boulders loose from the cliff above, and they crash around us with a dull, neck-snapping thud. Thunder smashes into the canyon, and I gain some insight into what a nail must hear when struck. Lightning ricochets off canyon walls. Trees swirl overhead in a blender of motion; branches crack and fall like spears..."

Q. What percent of visitors to Bryce Canyon National Park go for a hike below the rim?
1) 10 percent   2) 25 percent   3) 40 percent
A. 3) About 40 percent. Bryce Canyon has about 65 miles (104 km) of hiking trails.

Rockfall results on Navajo Loop Trail in Wall Street, Bryce Canyon National Park

Q. With all the fragile-looking hoodoos at Bryce Canyon, do they ever fall on the trails?
A. Yes, almost every year a rock fall closes a trail for a while. In the spring of 2010, a rock fall in the Wall Street section of the Navajo Loop Trail kept it closed for several months.

Q. Do rocks ever fall on people?
A. Almost. The rock fall in Wall Street in 2010 scraped the foot of a girl. In 2006 another rock fall in Wall Street fell right between two groups of people. But no one has been killed on a Bryce Canyon trail. Most injuries are caused by people wearing footwear with inadequate treads, and they slip and fall on the loose gravel and dirt, even breaking ankles or legs.

When peregrine falcons are nesting on Zion cliffs in springtime, nearby climbing routes are closed.

Q. Does the National Park Service remove dangerous hoodoos before they fall?

A. In most cases, even a geologist finds it hard to predict when a Bryce Canyon hoodoo or a Zion cliff will fall. A precarious-looking hoodoo might last 200 years, while a solid-looking cliff might fall tomorrow morning. People come to national parks to see nature in action, even if that involves a bit of risk.

Q. What recreational activity is very popular at Bryce Canyon, but hard to do at Zion?

A. Cross-country skiing and snowshoeing. Bryce Canyon

Snowingshoeing Bryce Canyon National Park's Fairyland Loop Trail

gets far more snow than Zion, and skiing can be the only way to get around. Bryce Canyon has over ten miles of ski trails, and there are many more miles of ski trails just outside the park. Ruby's Inn sponsors a winter festival with ski races and ice sculptures. The hoodoos are especially beautiful when coated with snow.

To avoid dehydration, rangers recommend drinking one gallon (3.8 liters) of water per day.

DEATH
IN ZION AND BRYCE CANYON

National parks are supposed to be all about beauty and peace, but occasionally they are the scene of tragic accidents. These accidents tend to get a lot of media attention, and this creates a lot of curiosity about accidents and deaths in national parks. The National Park Service makes use of this curiosity to educate the public to avoid dangers. Many park visitors are out of their familiar environments, and simply don't recognize the dangers of events like flash floods or lightning. Most deaths in national parks could be prevented by a bit of education and care.

Q. Who was the first person to die unnaturally at Zion or Bryce Canyon?
A. Undoubtedly it was a Native American, but we'll never know exactly who, when, or how. Canyon country is a tough environment, even for those who know it well. Even Native Americans fell off cliffs, got attacked by mountain lions, or counted on finding water at a spring that had dried up. They too had a sense of adventure, which occasionally got them into trouble. When Don Orcutt climbed Zion's Great White Throne in 1931, he said he found a human skull there, perhaps a Native American who

climbed the peak only to discover he couldn't get back down. (A few months later, Orcutt fell and died while trying to climb Cathedral Mountain.) A few days before Nephi Johnson became the first Euro-American to enter Zion Canyon, a bear killed some Paiute hunters there. The first white settlers near Zion heard the story of a Paiute who was climbing the ancient steps carved into the steep slope above Weeping Rock, but he fell and was killed.

Q. Who was the first Euro-American to die unnaturally in Zion?
A. It didn't take long for Zion to claim its first Euro-American victim. Mormon pioneers were building the first wagon road into Zion Canyon in the winter of 1864–1865, digging a cut through a slope near the river. They didn't have any blasting powder, so they had to use shovels to dig out boulders and roll them away. George Ayers and Orson Taylor stopped to rest beside a boulder they were digging out, when the boulder suddenly broke loose and rolled onto George Ayers, crushing and killing him.

Q. Who was the first person to die in Zion after it became a national park?
A. In April, 1930, eleven years after Zion became a national park, a local school teacher, Albin Brooksby, took his kids to visit Weeping Rock. The abandoned and decaying structure of the cable works was still there, and a piece of metal from one of the rusting baskets fell on Brooksby and killed him. Because of this accident, the remains of the cable works were removed. This wasn't the first tragedy connected with the cable works. Atop the canyon rim the metal cable and its metal structures attracted a lot of lightning. In July of 1908 two youths from Springdale were visiting a friend who worked at the cable works when all three were struck by lightning, which killed two of them.

Q. Who was the first tourist to die in Zion National Park?
A. It was a 19-year-old youth from St. Louis, who was staying at Zion Lodge in 1930. Alone, he ascended the Lady Mountain Trail near the Emerald Pools. Built in 1925, the Lady Mountain Trail was a very steep route, involving ladders, 1,400 steps cut into the rock, and over 1,000 feet of cables. After reaching the top, he attempted to descend, possibly in the dark. He strayed off the

---

Zion's Esplin Gulch was named for Lynn Esplin, who made its first descent searching for lost sheep, but died there.

trail and fell to his death. After many years of accidents, the Lady Mountain Trail was closed and dismantled in the 1970s.

Around 1947 a woman on a bus tour disappeared from Zion Lodge. Searchers failed to find her anywhere. Two weeks later a Los Angeles policeman was vacationing in Zion, and at the Emerald Pools he smelled an odor he recognized. He found the woman's corpse. She had a bullet hole through her skull. Nearby was her torn-up tour ticket, and when police pieced the ticket back together, they discovered her name. On checking, they discovered that the woman had a terminal illness. Her death was ruled a suicide. Perhaps she had chosen to die in a beautiful place.

Q. Which is deadlier in Zion National Park: flash floods, or falls from trails?
A. Falls, by a large margin. While records are incomplete, as of 2010 nine persons are known to have died from flash floods in Zion National Park, and 35 are known to have died by falling from trails.

Q. What's the deadliest trail in Zion National Park?
1) Angels Landing   2) Emerald Pools
3) Hidden Canyon
A. 1) Angels Landing, which has claimed 11 lives as of 2010. The Emerald Pools Trail has claimed seven lives. Several other trails have each taken two lives. As with other national parks, a large portion of the falling deaths in Zion National Park involve young males, who are trying to show off, or taking foolish chances.

Emerald Pools waterfalls during high water in the spring

Q. Which is deadlier in Zion National Park: falls from trails, or falls from climbing the cliffs?
A. Falls from trails, by far. Compared with 35 known fatal falls

---

At the top of the Emerald Pools waterfall, people have slipped on the wet rocks and been swept over the falls.

from trails as of 2010, there have been only four recorded fatal falls involving climbers.

Canyoneering in Zion has resulted in many more deaths than climbing. One example is a 20-year-old woman who was canyoneering in Lodge Canyon, behind Zion Lodge, in 1999. When her rope became jammed in a cliff, she tried to free it, but she dislodged a rock, causing her to lose her balance. She fell 150 feet (46 m) to her death.

Zion National Park has one of the best search-and-rescue teams in the National Park Service, but sometimes even they face daunting challenges. In 1992  a man was trying to rappel into a slot canyon when the small tree onto which he'd attached his rope pulled loose, and he fell about 30 feet (9 m). He was now lying 150 feet (46 m) below a rocky keyhole opening only 20 feet (6 m) wide. By the time rescue rangers arrived in a helicopter, it was night. Using night-vision goggles, they hovered over the keyhole. The helicopter rotor blades swirled only a dozen feet (4 m) above the rocks. They lowered a cable into the keyhole, like threading a rock needle, until it reached the bottom. Then they hoisted the victim through the keyhole. The victim was still alive, but soon he died.

Q. True or false: people can die in a flash flood even when there isn't a cloud in the sky.
A. True. Canyons can stretch dozens of miles and drain plateaus far beyond that, so a local but intense thunderstorm can create a flash flood that travels many miles from where the rain fell, and travels for hours after the rain stopped. The Zion Narrows has a drainage of 400 square miles (1,040 sq. km), and all the rain that falls in this area has to squeeze through cliffs only 20 feet (6 m) wide, so water can rise fast, high, and furious.

In 1986, a bicycle crash in the Zion-Mt. Carmel Tunnel killed the bike rider.

"The flood began as a trickle, first over our shoe tops. Then came what appeared to be a great wave of hay. It was pine needles. Then came the roar and finally, the trees and brush and boulders. It all happened almost within seconds." And just as fast, five people had died in the Zion Narrows. These five were part of a group of 26 people hiking the Narrows in September 1961, when they were caught in a downpour and a 10-foot-high (3 m) flood. One of the victims was spotted because his legs were sticking out of a pile of driftwood in Springdale. Two of the other victims were never found.

At age 14, Roger Clubb was already a famous climber. In 1941 Roger and his father Merrel Clubb made the first ascent of Cheops Pyramid, one of the tall, steep buttes inside the Grand Canyon. In 1946 Roger, now age 19, and his father made the first ascent of Vishnu Temple, one of the most challenging routes in the Grand Canyon. These feats probably gave Roger a bit of overconfidence. Later that summer Roger, now working as a cook at Zion Lodge, attempted to climb the Great White Throne. When two of his friends turned back, Roger continued alone. But he miscalculated the time, and ended up spending the night on a tiny ledge, using his belt to tie himself to a bush. Rangers came to his rescue. Zion's superintendent then proposed permanently banning climbing from the park, but the director of the National Park Service disagreed. Seventeen years later, in 1963, Roger Clubb took his eight-year-old son on a hike into the Grand Canyon. A flash flood caught them. Roger could have saved himself, but he rushed to rescue his son, and both were killed. These were the first recorded flash-flood deaths in the history of Grand Canyon National Park.

Q. In April, 2010, two young men from Las Vegas tried to build a raft out of logs and float through the Zion Narrows. The river was running high and cold—about 40 F (4 C). They didn't wear wetsuits or lifejackets, and had no rafting experience. They had little food or camping gear. Their raft broke up, and they drowned. Their

67 people have died from flash floods in the state of Utah.

bodies were found below the Narrows. Why were they trying to raft the river?

1) To win a bet

2) To film themselves for a reality TV show

3) To escape the police

A. 2) To film themselves for a reality TV show.

Zion-Mt. Carmel Highway construction, about 1930

Q. Was anyone killed in the building of the Zion-Mt. Carmel Highway and Tunnel?

A. Two workers died, one in a rockslide on the switch-backs, and the other inside the tunnel, from inhaling a toxic mixture of sand and dynamite fumes. In 1959, when motorists could still stop in the galleries inside the tunnel, a 42-year-old woman fell out of a gallery and down 200 feet (61 m) to her death.

Q. Have there been any plane crashes at Zion or Bryce Canyon?

A. On July 11, 1973, an Air Force F-111 jet crashed into Deertrap Mountain, which is above Zion Lodge. The pilots ejected and survived. Some wreckage from the jet is still on the slopes. In October 1947, Bryce Canyon was the site of a commercial airline crash that, in number of fatalities, is tied for the worst in American history up to that time. A United DC-6 was flying from Los Angeles to Chicago when a design flaw caused a fire, which burned through the tail section. The pilots tried to make an emergency landing at the Bryce Canyon airport, just outside the park, but the tail section came off and the plane crashed. The crash killed all 53 people on board, including a baby who was born as a result of the crash but who took only one breath. This crash was the first time in aviation history that a plane was reconstructed from its debris to determine the cause of a crash. This crash was the first inside any national park, and remains the worst in Utah history.

Since 1950, about 50 people have been killed by lightning in Utah.

Q. What causes the most deaths at Bryce Canyon?
1) Falls   2) Lightning   3) Heart attacks
A. 3) Heart attacks. Bryce Canyon's high altitude and thin air can place extra stress on hearts, especially on a steep trail. Take it easy!

Q. Bryce Canyon's high altitude also makes it a dangerous place for lightning. In the state of Utah, Bryce Canyon is the second-worst place for lightning fatalities. How often do people get hit by lightning there?

1) One per year   2) Two per year   3) One every two years
A. 3) One every two years. One out of three people hit by lightning have died. In the 25 years between 1985 and 2010, four people were killed. One of these fatalities was an 18-year-old employee at Bryce Canyon Lodge; the lodge lobby contains a plaque in her honor. Another victim was standing in the middle of a crowd of people, but everyone else survived. One survivor had his gold necklace melted right into his skin. Lightning hits hoodoos and tears off rocks. Lightning often hits trees, killing many of them. As you walk along the rim you can see long scars running down many trees. In some areas, one of every five trees has been hit by lightning. Trees can't flee from lightning, but humans can. The safety rule is that if you see lightning and you hear its thunder within 30 seconds, you are too close and should seek shelter. Shelter does not mean standing under trees; this might keep you drier, but it also makes you a much better target for lightning.

In general, the #1 killer of outdoor adventurers is hypothermia.

About the Author

Don Lago started exploring Zion and Bryce Canyon in the 1980s, and he was happy to explore them in more depth for the sake of this book. He is the author of *Grand Canyon Trivia* and *Death Valley Trivia*, both also released by Riverbend Publishing. He has spent 25 years exploring the Grand Canyon as a hiker, a kayaker, and a historian. His first visit to a national park was to Yosemite at age four, although his main memory of that visit is the Yogi Bear coin bank he bought there. Since then, his appreciation of the national parks has only increased. Lago is well-known for his writing on nature, astronomy, and history, which have appeared for many years in magazines such as *Orion, Astronomy,* and *Air and Space Smithsonian.* He has published several books on astronomy and history.

Q. Where can you get answers to hundreds of questions about your favorite national parks?
A. In the National Parks Trivia Series!